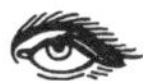

CANCELLED CONFESSIONS

CLAUDE CAHUN

CANCELLED CONFESSIONS

(or Disavowals)

ILLUSTRATED WITH
PHOTOMONTAGES
COMPOSED BY
MARCEL MOORE
AND CLAUDE CAHUN

ORIGINAL PREFACE
BY PIERRE MAC ORLAN

Aveux non Avenus translated
from the French by Susan de Muth

with an essay by Amelia Groom

siglio 2025

Front and back cover image: detail from the photomontage for chapter II, "MOI-MÊME," [myself] by Claude Cahun and Marcel Moore
Cover and book design: Natalie Kraft

Siglio is grateful to the Jersey Heritage Trust for creating digital files of the photomontages from the original glass plate negatives, providing the images reproduced here and their kind assistance, and to Thin Man Press for their generosity in helping to realize this edition. Thanks as well to Eugenie Dalland, Martha Ormiston and Elizabeth Zuba.

First printing | ISBN: 978-1-938221-36-1
Printed and bound in Lithuania by Balto

siglio *uncommon books at the intersection of art & literature*
po box 234, south egremont, massachusetts 01258
sigliopress.com p: 310-857-6935

Available in North America to the trade through D.A.P./Artbook.com
75 Broad Street, Suite 630, New York, NY 10004
p: 212-627-1999 f: 212-627-9484

Susan de Muth would like to thank Agnès Lhermitte, writer and educator, for her patient explanations and intelligent interpretations of some of the more obscure words, references and passages in the original French text. Thanks are equally due to Hannah Freed-Thall and Amelia Groom who have been exceptionally generous in sharing their knowledge and expertise, contributing much wide-ranging advice, information and support to the preparation of this volume.

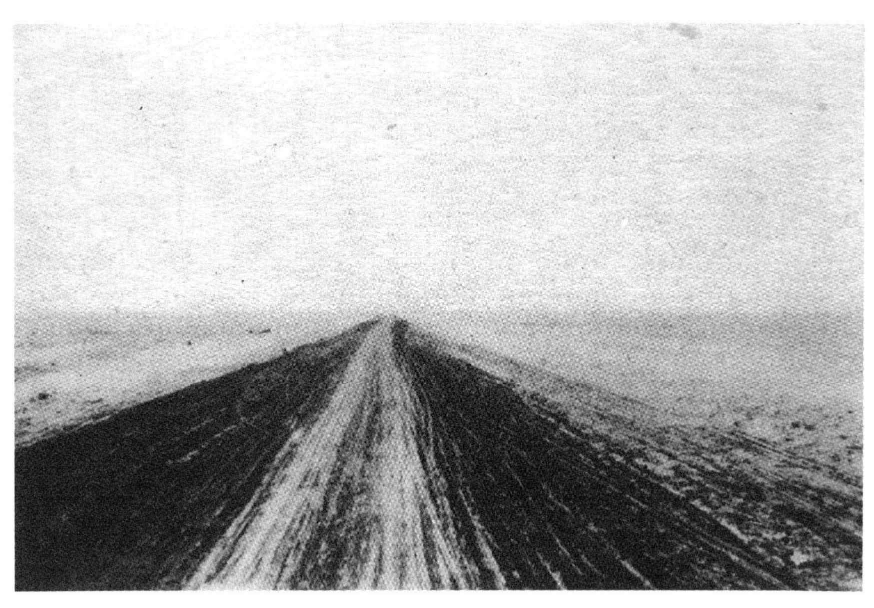

TABLE

CANCELLED CONFESSIONS (or Disavowals)

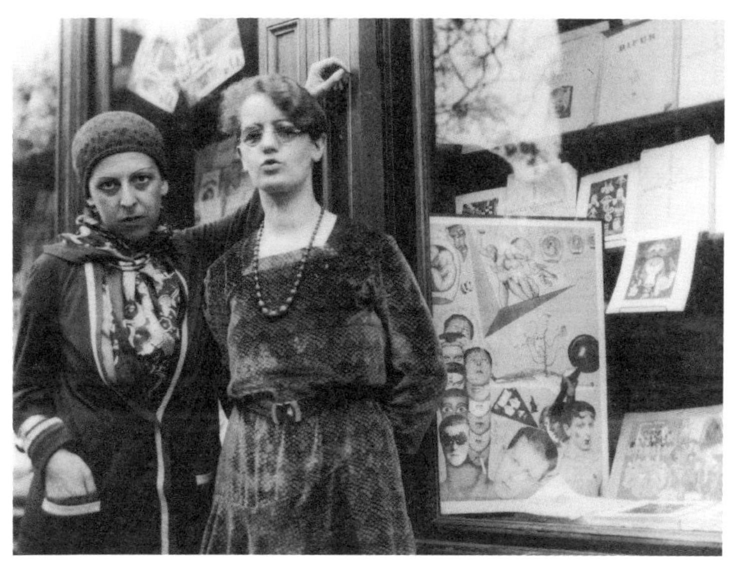

Previous spread: on the left, a reconstruction in English of the original table of contents; on the right, a photograph of Claude Cahun and an unidentified woman outside the José Corti bookshop, 6 rue de Clichy, 1930, photographer unknown (note the display of works from *Aveux non Avenus* in the window). Image courtesy of the Jersey Heritage Trust.

Opposite: a replication of the original front cover of *Aveux non Avenus* (the back cover can be found at the end of the text on page 232).

CLAUDE CAHUN

AVEUX NON AVENUS

ÉDITIONS DU CARREFOUR

MCMXXX

A *Preface to* Cancelled Confessions

Introducing these pages is a difficult task. Where the aim of literature is to set itself free, it virtually eludes all criticism, particularly that of professional critics.

Mademoiselle Claude Cahun, the niece of the author of Vies Imaginaires,[1] *has inherited a state of torment so richly productive that one should not wish her rid of it.*

This book is virtually entirely dedicated to the word "adventure." Perhaps one should consider exactly how the author would define this word.

I think that the adventure here is, by its very nature, interior, but it is presented to us in a series of cinematic glimpses which insist on the cerebral, rather than plastic, nature of the enterprise.

This almost cruel poem is infused with a very peculiar light, emanating from emotional ingredients of perfectly human origin. The undeniably fantastic beauty of these images furthermore has at its heart a series of feelings perfectly common to all, such as love when it hasn't quite shaken off melancholy.

It is love that gives the street its deep melancholy; the extraordinary mutability of love imbues the art of photography with infinite mystery.

The great emotional valets of our age are the camera and the gramophone.

Both have appropriated for themselves a little of the celestial fire so many men have sought with an often infantile sensuality.

The emotional life that Claude Cahun brings into her domain — the adventure — can be contained in a dozen records known only to herself.

The gramophone is an instrument of poetic control. A poetic mirror. It cannot be put into just any hands.

I sometimes see aspects of Isabelle Eberhardt[2] in Claude Cahun; I know that this impression is not totally correct, but this literary resemblance is a cerebral creation, born of the association of the gramophone and the camera.

If the talking machine did not recreate the world more or less daily, it would have no greater function than to replace an ensemble of instruments. Its poetic import would be no greater than that of a bandstand between five and seven.

We know that this is not the case.

The sum total of poem-essays and essay-poems contained in this publication — which is not a slim volume — is the equivalent of the more or less regulation 300 pages of an adventure novel conceived to conform to public taste. Ideas trace elegant parabolas to end in a tragic unfolding, exploding without a sound.

I believe that each idea this author launches forms a trajectory parallel to that of her own life. To comment too precisely on this book would be almost indiscreet.

The characters that evolve in this funeral procession are not exactly phantoms. More exactly, these are apparitions whose weight, nonetheless, can be calculated, who cannot evade the touch of a hand.

Claude Cahun is a wandering writer. She progresses irresistibly through the night, a night full of lights to which she gives the names of people, the names of plants, the names of shellfish.

This night broods over a strange congress of sometimes tender, sometimes furious forms and ideas. A philosophical orchestra plays discreetly.

At dawn, all of this disappears. And on the unadorned shoreline, a shoreline more naked than an operating table, all that will remain is a female corpse polished like a marble statue and near it, as if escaped from a breast for which it has no further use, a firm and mobile heart, obviously living, with all its complicated machinery clear to see.

Pierre Mac Orlan, 1930

1919 – 1925

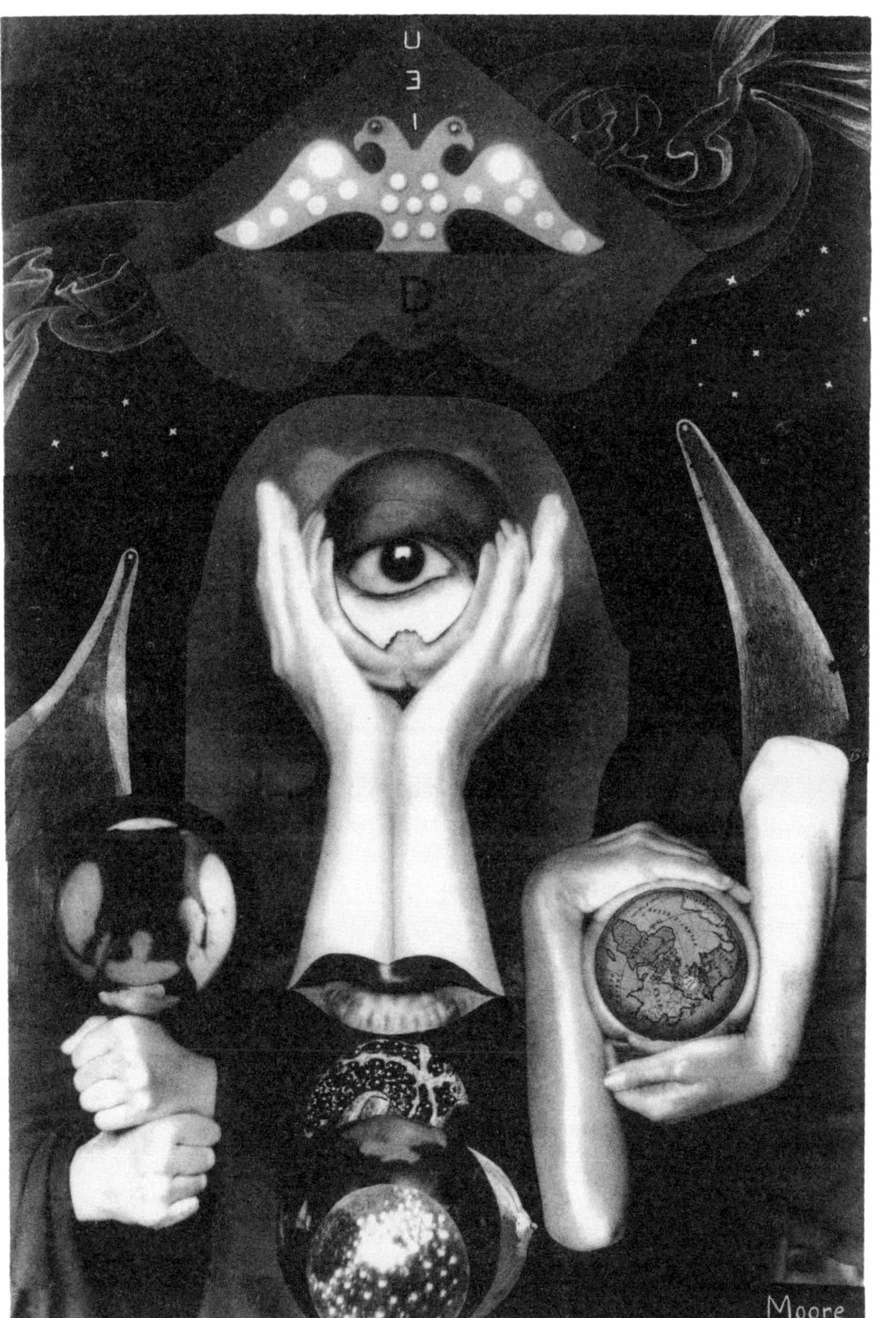

The invisible adventure.

The lens tracks the eyes, the mouth, the wrinkles skin deep...
The expression on the face is fierce, sometimes tragic. And then
calm — a knowing calm, worked on, flashy. A professional smile —
and voilà!

The hand-held mirror reappears, and the rouge and eye shadow.
A beat. Full stop. New paragraph.

I'll start again.

To those who know nothing of the steps, obstacles and enormous
chasms I've leapt over — and I've revealed none of it — this all must
seem the most ludicrous merry-go-round.

Should I then burden myself with all the paraphernalia of facts,
stones, cords delicately cut, precipices... It doesn't interest me at all.
Guess, recover. Vertigo is implied, ascension or the fall.

To please them, would you have to follow the unknown woman,
step by step, illuminating her up to the ankle? Heels worn down,
mud, feet bleeding — these humble and truthful testaments — they
would surely touch somebody's heart. Whereas...

No. I'll trace the wake of vessels in the air, the pathway over the
waters, the pupils' mirage.

No point in making myself comfortable. The abstraction, the dream, are as limited for me as the concrete and the real. What to do? Show a part of it only, in a narrow mirror, as if it were the whole? Mix up a halo with spatters? Refusing to bump into walls, bump into windows instead? In the black of night.

Until I see everything clearly, I want to hunt myself down, struggle with myself. Who, feeling armed against their own self, be it even with the vainest of words, would not do their very best if only to hit the void bang in the middle.[3]

It's false. It's very little. But it trains the eye.

Only with the very tip would I wish to sew, sting, kill. The rest of the body, what comes after, what a waste of time! Only ever travel in the prow of myself.

I

R. C. S.

At just seven years old, without realizing it, I was already looking for sentimental adventure, driven — as I am now — by impotence, with all the strategic impudence that characterizes me still.

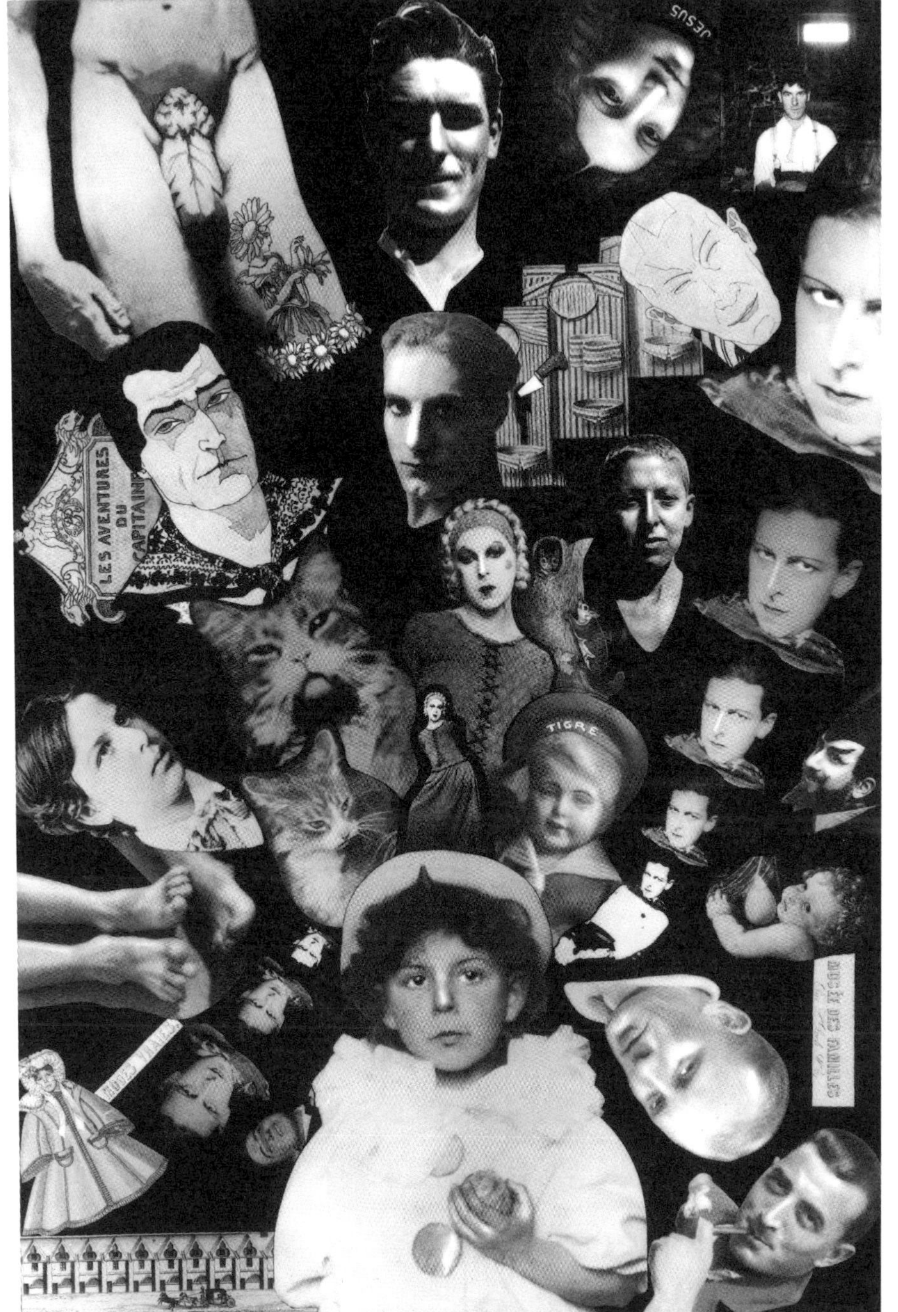

JESUS
LES AVENTURES DU CAPITAINE
TIGRE
MUSÉE DES FAMILLES

Time Change.

> He: So what!
> Me: So what!
> The other: What a life...

Indiscreet and brutal, I enjoy looking at what's underneath the crossed-out bits of my soul. Ill-advised intentions have been revised there, become dormant; others have materialized in their place.

I love whisky: it's unpleasant — you don't feel as though you're committing a sin; and it's strong — it makes you drunk. This evening I got myself about a liter of the stuff. I got into bed; the lights are low and my little debauchery within easy reach. I'm drinking and smoking and writing to kill all my feelings. The slovenliness of my race.[4]

I'm thinking about Bob, of course, Bob at the bar.[5] My cheeks produce dimples — they're fake yet a competent imitation. — Bob... This is a truly intellectual love. Who'd believe it? — Who? Who would I want to fool into believing it? You[6] know all about it: I explain everything to you, exaggerate. Your absence is an illusion. Fifteen years of intimacy aren't shaken off with a bit of tobacco, some alcohol and a few words. In vain do I refuse to name you, my familiar witness. The mind will never get out of the rut it's in, memory will never burst its hinges,[7] spring from its grave, nor will my heart come out of its shell.

I can only read about others between your lines... — Icarus?[8] O memory still-born. — Saccard?[9] I envied him, admired his energy to such an extent that I forgot he does not actually use it for anything superhuman. I would have given my soul away easily, too easily (clearly it doesn't weigh much), and thrown my body in for good measure — a free gift. However chastely, however humbly this was done they wanted nothing to do with either. My only excuse — your forgiveness — lies in this unexpected outcome (O desires without repentance! Will you ever end, O scornful fatalism of the sage despite himself?): a death, a will, a sincere life, all spurned... O dried-up sensualities, sensualities of the summer! — Am I not twenty-six years old? — No! Already! — In this Indian summer? A heat unique in the annals of astronomy. — Ah! What am I saying? What was I saying? Memories in madness. (O unrepentant regrets — and how you whine! Why don't you shut up? In the absence of other lips, gnaw your own to pulp...) Eyes over there — depths — dream-filled looks, never fixed; here, mouths — abysses — and so well adapted: safety rails prevent folly. All falling strictly forbidden.

Ledunois, Pyrrhus,[10] sometimes even Arcadius?[11] Sensual complicity only... Complicity?[12] She's a funny one, O impossible me! Am not I among all people — no: like all people, to put it correctly! — alone, eternally alone. Let's brag about it, let's hurry: we have no other death insurance.

Diomedes?...[13] He passes. He's already in night right up to his neck and I'm coming too late. I can feel that he's lost. He's dug his own grave. Could I fill it in? Let's leave burrowing to timid rabbits... — And Bob again, did he see? Anguish. Who's calling me? My face hardens, visibly hardens. Masks my weakness. Pride: I'm like him. Enough: I'm giving him up. How easy it is from afar. I'll say it again and again until my heart capitulates to the starvation of boredom's lengthy siege. I was Prince for awhile and cannot think about it without pretensions of nobility. Nobility! And Bob again. How obvious his royalty was to me! That love, so intellectual! To the point of debauchery, to the point of absurdity. Only the others saved me from harm. I'd have gaily thrown my soft, warm body into the merciless fire for them, for some among them, for him in any case. But entering Hell held out no hope for me...

O you, you whom I love — you who tolerate my love when all is said and done — one and only God, I would never even have dared say I miss you...

And this infernal red ring next to my flickering lamp, — O whisky! — gliding through the green sky bottle, descending, faltering... Will I finish it?

Intellectual passions. Yes, I assure you. Equal in strength. Weight — let's be modest — average. Yes, it's a contest — You, (woe to the conquered!)[14] emperor-gladiator supreme, Saint John the Baptist[15] finger pointing up — pointing down, for all things are relative and I am looking down — be cruel, cruel. I feel as if I'm dying, (feebly) dying — but I know very well that it's an illusion. In fact, it's a habit I adopt to endure and make others endure the vital force of a vicious beast. Let's be cruel. It's not dangerous...

He'll be defeated. I want my revenge. He'll be... I want him... O Fortune, O sorrow! What's to be done? He won't have me. And what about me? Do I really want him? Yes? No? — I don't know for sure...

I've got everything ready. Nothing is missing. Hurry up you lower classes![16] No, I'll show you all the door... — I've had enough: I want to die. Isn't that the very best recovery? — I want to live. Ah, I've already said it. I'm losing my memory. Or am I already drunk? No, sorrow is prowling and howling inside me like a wild beast in a cage. The cage is not very strong — let the curious beware. It's going, I'm going to... you...

It's nothing. Shut up, shut up! Let's be silent; let's be... — let's not be. Or simply, gently passive beneath his impassive spade like a naked furrow,[17] dug, turned over, gaping flesh, where wild weeds...[18] (Vegetable life. Love in slow motion...) wild, wave only as he permits. But you crazy woman! He doesn't permit even that...

— Damn! Down with all this submission. Let's be as plentiful as the earth — bountiful and superficially cultivated, of course.

I was trained for you. By whom? Defying what? Nothing, O submission. I am positively outraged! I'm losing my memory, and this vague personality crumbles having been tricked into building it-self up too much. I'll dissociate myself from it completely if someone gives me another... But enough of this. Let's dissolve.

I love you. That should be enough for the whole solar system. I love you and another too. Oh! this shameful plural, little prostituted soul. Does it imagine that the verb acquires by this a more numerous strength of conviction? My soul? The bitch! It's less pure than my body... (You will already have come to that conclusion. Forgive me: my spirit is weak... but the flesh is willing!), and more feminine — What can I do? Ah! Wear it out.

Individualism? Narcissism? Certainly. My best characteristic, the one and only intentional fidelity I am capable of. You don't care? I'm lying anyway: I scatter myself too widely for that.

I despair. I love him with physical abandon — this fantasy knows no respite — with all my soul...[19] He doesn't care. It's true. I totally understand it! Will he want my passion if I leave it to him in my will? Passion... and mine will improve with age, admirable wine that will lose its kick. — Ageless water might be preferred. He won't want it. And he'll be right. Would I want it if the law allowed you to bequeath things to yourself, dying so that you would belong to yourself?

Is it all by chance?... No. I only believe in what I want. I can believe in the impossible, for example: That God, you and I are one and the same place, that hell, paradise and my sheets merge together, that the instant, the eternal, my syllables long and short are (correctly pronounced) one and the same word.

I loved him. He didn't resist. Our lives should have become simpler.

But the severe god, that furious, childish artist, snapped his arrow[20] of potential perfection and separated us:

It was too easy a harmony!

Fast and good.

Short but sweet.

Our bodies met from knees to shoulders. An arm, all trembling, explored my heart, and I was ashamed of the irregular breathing that betrayed my desire...

Compulsion, a stranger to love, kept us thus, glued against one another in the midst of indifference. Yet we gave ourselves totally, hastily and with great ardor, in an intonation, a look, the lightest touch concentrating stiffening tissue. Together we greedily delighted in the abandon of our connection — maintained as best we could through the bumps of the machine. (Wasn't it a motor race against the clock: a twenty-minute pretext for all this? How did I have time to notice any of this? — But I didn't of course: I must have been told afterwards!). Rigid abandon, not in the least inconsistent, conscious, wished for...

Would our loving wills[21] destroy each other in the end, with an equal magnetism exerting too much strain? When the appropriate moment came, we separated without so much as touching hands.

And the family finds this natural! — Natural, certainly; animal for sure; but appropriate, humane? For me, it was too much! — or too little. Ah!... To relive each sensation in detail, for the totality escaped me. It was so much! And so little in truth. What was I saying about "natural"?... If we were two dogs, two unsociable cats, we'd at least have possessed each other before sacrificing ourselves to the routine of our ferocious assertions of individuality. With pleasure I imagine my body exhausted, satisfied, with no expectation that my soul would return and recoil.

I'm stopping here. I don't know how to go on. My unfulfilled desire, in its most abstract form, is now nothing more than a mechanical expression of my thought, a litany like the songs of idiots. I despise it.

Calm me, little brother.

Jersey, September 20, 1920.
(Letter)

... Yesterday (an enduring yesterday — if it isn't today's, it's very like it), I was up and about, by chance and by habit, on the road to nowhere, meditating without hope, without any faith in myself, in you and above all in him, and with no charitable feeling towards anything.

Despising all my plans, despising the cowardice that prevents me from putting them into action even more. (I came for this pointless conquest and will not leave without having accomplished it... or without having smashed every chance of an attempted embrace. To crush a lasting happiness with the slightest simple touch, to disarm a dream as yet unrealized with one single disappointed touch. To the point of laughter, O my wounded mouth... Maybe I will draw some tears from you and I will do him harm. There will be some curious ricochets. I was born to create my own misery, the prolonged boredom and the brief disdain of you others!) Above all else, I despised the way I despise myself...

Little by little a murmur seizes me by the entrails; voices caress my ears, become distinctive (I won't turn my head), take up their positions (the rest of my effort deployed in calculating the distance

— distance already diminishing), speak (*Till we meet again*), catch up with me and pass me (just). An abrupt halt, military, with salute and clicked heels on the decisive syllable.

All my bitterness, alas! and all my wild resolution abandons me. On this, of all evenings, he should not have come: no smile has illuminated his face for five full circles of the sun (he has the right to spurn my tenderness, only that), and the nocturnal tide bears the gloomy rain of morning back against us. On this of all evenings, though no longer really expected, here he is. His eager laughter that I find so refreshing, his breath like a strong wind dries out my clenched soul. Though my heart feels completely the opposite, my words of welcome are rough, lashing him as they force their way out of my soft, contracted mouth; my eyes are shining and burning with the tears they have not shed...

Did I ever once show him any anger, or malice, despite this week of suffering? I never had any such intention. But sometimes, living within us unnoticed, words which nothing has invited — a whole hostile crowd — make use of our lips.

Shining under the downpour, his black oilskin with the wide collar, the sleeves over his fingers, lend him the sublime air of a Prophet (prophet of Himself alone). Before me, his righteous pride like a royal coat.

Even conceding my defeat would no longer please me, from now on I wish to live in the midst of bristling incertitude. I want to expose myself, bare-headed, to the sudden showers of an eternal Springtime.

All that exists for me is that moment and the one that followed it in terms of logic, if not time. What does chronology matter?

Sweet though, beneath a candle stuck in an old bottle of Bass, the moment when our two heads (ah! that our hair would meld indistinguishably) leaned together over a photograph. Portrait of one or the other, our two narcissisms drowning there, it was the impossible realized in a magic mirror. The exchange, the superimposition, the fusion of desires. The unity of the image achieved through the close friendship of two bodies — for the sake of which they send their souls to the devil!

Not their souls, but what serves them as such, not these solemn sisters, but this everyday consciousness: the intellect, happiness, stability, well-established love, memories, habits, the future, becoming.

Postscript: At present I exist otherwise.

Ah, the inevitable.

O sweet little girl, leave the dried flower of your grace between the leaves of my books and my favorite acts, may I become accustomed to your scent whose insipidity still faintly nauseates me, whose bitter drunkenness — and how I love it! — suffocates me at first, despite myself...

O pug-nosed death,[22] your immutable mold fearsomely forces itself onto aquiline-nosed faces.[23] This is why men of this type fear you more than any other. Be inflexible, implacable mask; remain rigid whether you wish to or not. Don't let yourself be insulted by me, little sweetness. Reclaim your pride, our queen. Not only decorative — you still are — but you were young and very modest once, and maybe you have remained so... Young, judging by your naivete, the blunders you commit on us — you are only learning, poor little thing! — and your likely immortality.

Life, death, ageless sisters. And yet the younger is you: you couldn't exist without your false twin, you are conjoined. You cannot exterminate her without destroying yourself.

But see how your hundred thousand victories an hour are valued: they are worth nothing more than your insignificant rival.

What does life do to defend herself? In poverty, she is mean; in wealth, vulgar; mutilated in asceticism; parasitical in faith; impotent and tortured in anarchy, continually subjected to interrogation; soiled in purity, prostituted, animal-like; a liar in heroism — or, from her very conception, constrained in giving you her word.

Renounce your influence, renounce yourself, O death, base death.

She.

I cannot.

Have an abrupt end? — Very well. But is death an unassailable rampart on top of a mountain or a simple parchment partition that the soul passes through like a bullet?

I hate it when sunlight or a loud noise roughly wrenches me from sleep in the morning.

Would I prefer to be brutally pushed out of life by silence and darkness falling?

To be abruptly awoken by a stranger in the other world?... — Ah! No.

The anguish of sleep.

Would I prefer silence and darkness falling...

Ah, how I envy those who are overcome by an unexpected sleep, the forehead suddenly struck and the head weighed down as if by a ball of lead! How happy too those children who are pushed into the unknown, never having uttered the oblivious birth cry of joy and pain! Ah, how I'd love to fall asleep like those good workers who die of old age, gently, tenderly, prepared for an effortless death by the continuous efforts of an undervalued life...

I lived in joyfulness; I wanted pleasure to be abrupt, a brutal awakening from the slightest drowsiness of the senses. All deathbeds are mine! I have won the right to struggle at the evening of each day as at the evening of life.

I remember, it was Carnival.[24] I had spent my solitary hours disguising my soul. Its masks were so perfect that when their paths crossed in the grand square of my consciousness they didn't recognize each other. Beguiled by their comic ugliness, I explored the worst possible instincts; I welcomed young monsters into myself and nurtured them. But the makeup I had used seemed indelible. I rubbed so hard to remove it that I took off all the skin. And my soul, like a flayed face, naked, no longer had a human form.

Like a dog, tethered by too short a rope, fretting, longing to be free in the sunshine, who surreptitiously gnaws at the hemp and flees into the countryside; like his heavy kennel — damp with soiled straw, retaining the odor, the imprint of the animal, its leftover food already rotting — can do nothing but wait, lost, too much impregnated with its presence for any other use to be tolerable — ready to be thrown on the fire; like my body, like my soul.

Like my insane soul, lost — oh, with no going back! — such easy prey.

Like my body, the undine's pure body, never soul-stained but violated by the beast, his mark, his scent, whatever he's chanced to eat, the traces of his meals — interpretations I have discarded, O memories already decomposing.

I can feel my thighs become thinner in the sweat of fever as if I could see it happening, sometimes a scalding shower, sometimes icy, always unexpected. My emptied knees, the bones dissolved, clothed in transparent parchment, blow up like floating pigs' bladders. My heart slows, tolls a mournful death knell, then beats noisily like an alarm. It starts to move around, wanders about in my stomach, bursts into it with agonizing cramps. With each contraction, a consciousness falls pulverized. Little by little I become lighter. Brief respite! My heart inflates outrageously, filling up with hydrogen. A massive red and blue balloon, it floats upwards at the end of a string.

At the other end is an imprisoned wasp which knocks at the walls of my breast with venomous blows. What if I helped it get out? And my nails would unhesitatingly tear a route to daylight for the fugitive from this heart were it not so despairingly dark outside.

O endless nocturne played in the circles of the musical night, infernal serpent which cut off its own head while swallowing its tail, bracelet with seven sealed chains...[25]

The red and blue balloon is so strong: it lifts me from my bed, mesmerized. I feel the loss of momentum in this levitation I have brought about, and the spectator's panic on realizing the danger. A sort of vague ecstasy sways me; and — remembering the abyss of sleep, underground vertigo interrupted by intermittent contractions, as crude as a fall — I indistinctly repeat:

I like ascending even more than descending. All will be well — up to the ceiling.

Once more I am master of my demons: I have understood.

I was at the edge of a beach with the tide rising. The waves of sleep wanted nothing to do with me and tossed me, shattered, onto the reefs of life.

I will stand upright on the dune, braced with the desire to fall, but blinded by the whiteness of a night of spume and sand.

Ah, I am really going mad![26] And Madness — O sickly mouth with infectious breath that ripped off my ear — in a monstrous voice prompts me with its poisonous doubt:

— When you lose your mind, does it start suddenly or gradually?

I repeat this docilely. And Madness looks at me with its staring eyes.

Docilely... my understanding ever more diminished, I surprise myself by saying:

— When you lose your consciousness, does it start suddenly or gradually?

Then, thoughtfully:

Will sleep take me in a spasm or will it stroke me, slowly and surely, with an eternal wing?...

There once was a rebellious child who no longer believed in sleep.

At first he had doubted God, and the concept of human liberty; then the material world and his own existence.

God had shrouded himself in mist, had disappeared from his heaven; the weakening of his will abandoned the field to instinct's whims; objects retained only a form, a color and the feel of dreams; their empire had fallen; no longer were they durable, solid or real. And the child began to merge with their disorder and lose his sense of self.

He had doubted love and love had targeted other, more passionate hearts. He even started to question dreams themselves, awake or sleeping; and sleep, gaudy as memories, white as ghosts, black as nothing; peopled sleep, deserted sleep; now an imitation of life, and now of death. He had already doubted life, now he doubted death itself.

And sleep came to take revenge for all of them: It came treacherously, slight and naked, twilight skin scarce brightened by hair the color of moon. A short dagger flashed in its clenched right fist. Under a rain of blows, the rebellious child shook with laughter, exposing his throat; no one so much as touched him. Without being aware of it, he had instinctively kept out of reach until now, resisting the lure of a deathly blade. But as he laughed, he closed his eyes. Sleep struck him a fatal blow, without malice — as if it were joking.

And death came, attracted by the odor of poppies. It touched the body nonchalantly and, without waking it, made of it a corpse.

Tuesday morning, seven o'clock
Jersey, September 21, 1920
(Letter)

... last night, tired of the rain, of myself, of an old English man who whispered your name and refused to understand, (refused, as they always do, to discuss anything properly), tired of Bob's too-long presence in the bar, of his absence, I smoked far too much. My heart started racing and clicked curiously on every beat — mysterious misfiring motor. On the verge of fainting, I lay down on a mattress which continually gives way. You know the feeling...

... then came sleep accompanied by the most hideous of its freed slaves: nightmares. To rid myself of these sempiternal supplicants, I deliver them unto you.

It was nighttime — but not very dark. A wan sky sickly freckled with stars. A northwester was raging in long, irregular gusts. I should have put out my cigarette because, walking westwards, the wind blew smoke, ash and even some tiny embers back into my eyes, onto my eyelids.

A group of sailors crossed my path. From their slurred speech and the fact that they didn't stop pissing as they walked along, rather than from their way of walking, I realized they were drunk. I turned my face away hoping that old Steel wasn't among them. I needn't have bothered: there was no mistaking the inimitable accent which uttered these words:

— Where did you find your left hand when you woke up this morning, my little lad?

To my horror, I heard his companion reply with the sweetness of a young girl:

— On top of my right of course, Sir!

They went by...

... And I soon found myself completely lost among a dense forest of lances coming out of deformed trunks, the blue of a dirty horizon. It was the army, on maneuver.

Then this mad, uncontrollable thought struck me like a well-aimed bullet:

"What folly to compulsorily arm all able-bodied men with lethal weapons and not subject their souls to an aptitude test!"

It's morning. After such a night, how could the sky look anything other than sick? A blotchy complexion and the sun obscured beneath eyelids with leaden dark circles.

The husky town crier of Croisic[27] just made an announcement. From the beach further down, where I am, his pot-bellied instrument looked as tall as a house to me.

— News: A child of thirty... rrr... three years old[28] has been killed in the parish of Guerande: Yves Claudanac. Information on the murderer, 26, rue Saint-Antoine. There will be a reward.

While this was going on, I saw all the spectators' suspicions manifest themselves, feature by feature on the drumskin, as if on a taut magic lantern screen, fade then reappear: the notorious thugs of the neighborhood, one of the child's uncles, who stood to inherit, and then the mother herself. The image of this lady persisted, disappearing one minute only to come back in a reconstruction of an imagined throat-slitting the next. This woman, passionate, irreligious and not much of a gossip, was locally taken for mad. She drew strange looks and prejudice. Since evidence of her innocence was not forthcoming, she was charged and imprisoned, while she repeated in a monotonous tone — like a cow ruminating — really having lost her head on this occasion:

— Yes, it was I who sent him to his death!

This was seen as a confession. And the Claudanac girl walked to the guillotine as if she were heading for the Promised Land, laughing through her tears...

— It's good she was condemned, someone said. She's only pretending to be mad.

What did this woman have left to live for? Yes, she was pretending, the crowd was right.

Does time beat truly in this broken-down old clock of a world? However impossible it might be, I have the impression that the other event — the other execution — occurs simultaneously.

A soldier is on guard on the ramparts. The glint of his bayonet wounds my mind. I've been rolling the little bullet they removed from the child's body in my pale palm for a long time — a bullet from a service revolver.

I go up to the sentry and borrow his weapon. Against all expectation he allows himself to be disarmed and shows no surprise. But before taking it to one side to check my inexplicable intuition, I could not prevent myself from addressing these incongruous words to him:

— Look, here is an old serrated kitchen knife you can use to defend yourself while I am gone...

A single bullet was missing from the revolver and the one I had fit perfectly — like Cinderella's glass slipper.

The rest is a matter for the courts. Let's just listen to the rapid confession of the guilty soldier:

"All my misfortune stems from the morbid taste for hunting rabbits my father encouraged from childhood...

"On the day in question I was idling on sentry duty when I caught sight of a small white moving dot, and I swear to you it was not much bigger than my usual target... No, I am not trying to excuse myself: it was a child and I knew it. I took aim nevertheless and hit the black center as accurately as if I was shooting at a paper target — and with scarcely more emotion. No, I am not trying to make myself out to be cynical...

"My misfortune had sprung from inside myself and you can do nothing about it. It started when I felt the blood come out of my veins, spilling all over my body, brimming over — worse than the way the river flooded this Spring! My arms were saturated in it, heavy and soggy. I was afraid to touch my face, anticipating its stickiness under my slimy fingernails; and I lifted my hands to the sky as high as I could — a truly involuntary prayer — for fear of seeing the hideous liquid I was floundering in — flooded, drowned, suffocating — ooze from them into the soil. I had made a hole in the earth like a cat when your men came to arrest me. And I was cleansing myself of all that nauseating filth of blood with this very knife...

"Don't make me wait for the guillotine, I entreat you!"

I went to the execution. I can testify that the wretch's blood flooded over the edge of the bucket and stained the public square with long criss-crossing rivulets. And everyone drew back for fear of being spattered.

The key to these dreams

The soldier's blood is just a symbol when it comes down to it: our minds pour themselves out in sleep. I am repelled by this dream and yet I hold on to it: it has the import of a Hilote[29] for me. Never lose your footing, introspection, consciousness. Madness is no less conceited than reason. The soul is an idiot that needs to be put in its place from time to time.

II

MYSELF

(for want of anything better)

The siren is beguiled by her own voice.

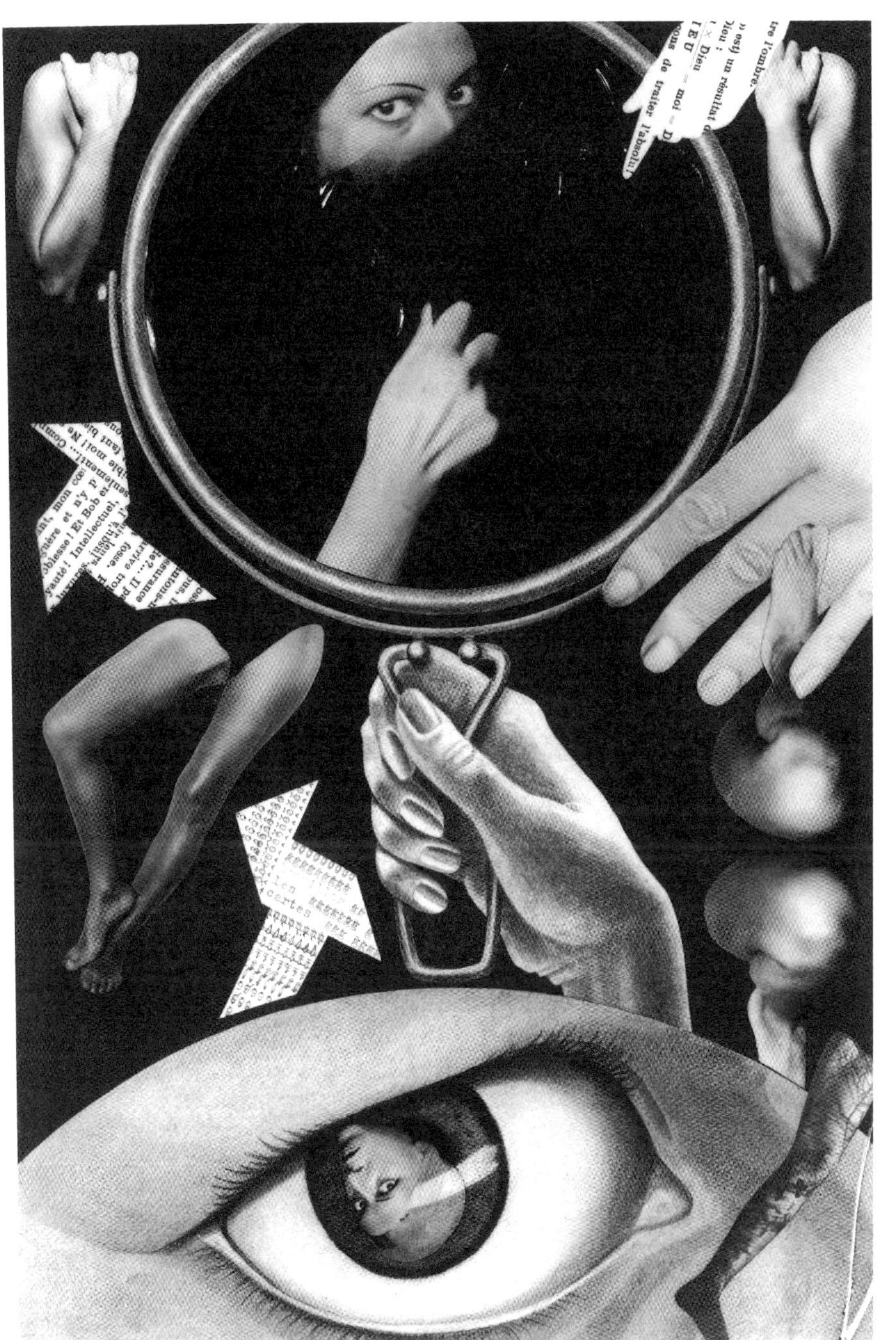

The sailors are far too occupied with navigating their vessel and the song of their flesh. The siren is the only victim of the siren. If later it is claimed she has overcome other prey, we will always recognize a romantic or commercial imperative: None is seized by her spells alone.

Anxious dawn.

Horizon lost in the waves' mist. Fragile, a crystal sky, a blue-gray sky...

(Her eyes become murky and fade; her breasts prowl and their roses of love, their pistils stand up.) — Sun, impatient beams!

Scarcely blue, on high the turquoises are dying. Flat and dappled, nippled, like fields of sand or emerald, gray dunes, pearl desert, monotonous morning already begun.

Perverse as a marine landscape, the child awakes and contemplates himself: Sad look! — Is it really necessary to live this wasted day?

False impressions.[30]

— Some more?
— No, thank you.
— This child is not greedy.
The child (off): I like better quality chocolates.

— Young girls, young boys?
— No, thank you.
— Are you celibate?
— Of course.
The young man, going back downstairs: Hades! Your flames are
not hot enough!

— He is modest (due to pride). — He lives simply (false luxury
disgusts him). — He is generous (because it's less easy to harm
courteously). — Intelligent (for want of anything better). — Likeable
(I have to be. For loneliness, alas, requires such physical and
spiritual munificence). — Discreet, tolerant, benevolent... (beware of
my ulterior motives!)

— He suffered with daring; he died without complaint... (I am a
masochist and I screamed so loudly with joy that your feeble human
ears couldn't hear a thing.)

Guillotine window.

A sheet of glass. Where shall I put the silver? Here or there; in
front of or behind the window?
In front. I imprison myself. I make myself blind. What does it
matter to me, Passerby, if I provide you with a mirror to see yourself
in, albeit a distorting mirror and signed by my own hand? I'm not

a dealer in mirrored wardrobes, or comical swing mirrors[31] (tragic, indeed; but banal tragedy. The ridiculous being a characteristic of man, it doesn't trouble me). Repellent attractions for the great fairground of human flesh...

Behind. I shut myself in just as much. I will know nothing of what is outside. At least I will know my face — and maybe that will be enough to please me.

Leave the window clear, and depending on chance and the hour see confusedly, partially, sometimes the fugitives and sometimes my gaze. Perfect reciprocity. (The one you know perfected the game, taking advantage of a "spy"). Clouded view, shattered lines... You don't want to stop, to understand. Can I do that myself?

So — break the windows but don't be low enough to call in the glazier. (He who makes up for his clumsiness pays for it.)

With the fragments, make a stained-glass window. Byzantine work.[32] Transparency, opacity. What an avowal of artifice! I will always end up pronouncing my own sentence. I told you: look at the sign — guillotine window...

May my serpent grip its tail between its teeth without letting go.

So then, abolish titles. They are keys. False modesty.

Express oneself: humiliate oneself? — Yes, but for the right reason.

Trample on this, this flesh of my flesh. Draw on remorse, weigh on my memory, on my obese statue, the only springboard that doesn't give way under me.

Is that shapeless, enormous, distressing, horribly voluptuous thing lying across my path? Opportunist soul: running over the body.

"Soul." I misused the word. Superstition, obsession with the unknowable. What I cannot chew is precisely what I like to bite off. "Love," "conscience," "God," "selflessness"!... I, Jewish to the point of using my sins for my salvation, of putting my by-products to work, of continually surprising myself, lockpick eye, on the edge of my own wastepaper basket.

And whatever I gather to myself, I will handle it with care, subjecting it to all my formulas, try out all my names, all my things on it, make room for it. My skeleton key will try all the locks. Can't it get any of them to open? I'll plant it there. Right in front of me.

It will still be of use. A wire, black or living, a stalk... A corolla of folded paper, a dress. A beautiful idol.

At the end of the day: laziness. For a moment I am happy with it. I stay where I am. You caught me in the throes of pride, groveling for so very little....

I close my eyes and await the visual lullaby. Hypnagogic image. My interpretation of it betrays me. So much the better: you only get a grip on yourself, only learn to see yourself through some spyhole.

In deep undergrowth roses, of whiteness pure and hard, hurl their blue thorns.

Behind, purple and violet leaves crowd in a dense mass, seemingly infinite, against which strutting flowers fan their tails, corollas preciously artless, alluringly artless: pale columbines, slightly pearly, lilies with disdainful pollen, Adonis flowers with stems that slim too suddenly, their growing too pliant and awkward.

Little foxgloves hatch along these stems, not sure whether to be flowers or pass for leaves, new leaves still chrysalids...

On moss blanched by shade, Prince Charming has condemned himself to sleep without cheating; to sleep while awaiting the deliverance worthy of his destiny, worthy of his proud virginity and through it, triumphant; to sleep forever.
(In the Garden of Pure Poisons[33] innocence, because easy — or rather, necessary — is terribly overrated, not to mention that it's too common there to be considered a virtue.)

Parsifal approaches the protective roses, he feels he was destined to awaken the Prince.[34]
(Now, Parsifal is as pure as anyone from the other side of the undergrowth can be: where merit is great, be it arduous and slow, imperfection persists.)

Thus the air without dust and the flowers without odor and the Prince's mouth full of absolute purities suffice and will long suffice to suffocate us, us and our foolhardy virtues.

Watertight bulkheads.

Ambition: to live without a support, as if of the plant species. Place one's ideal in oneself, sheltered from the elements.

It's all about converging lines. They don't meet for long. Where they stop is arbitrary. Continue to bring these lines to life, each in its own direction: you will correctly call them divergent.
Two parallel lines meet at infinity... How obliging words are!... It's the verbosity of bad friends, those who, knowing very well that they are failures, defeated in advance, incapable of giving us

happiness here below, offer it to us in abundance elsewhere, aleatoric, opening an easy credit account for us with no guarantee of heaven in the afterlife.

It has been said that you shouldn't become too attached to the body because beauty is nothing more than a play of light. Ephemeral. Illusory. What to say about the soul then? I understand others body and soul.

You should attach body and soul to yourself. Equilibrium. You change at the same time as yourself. You wouldn't know how to cheat on yourself. You walk in your own footsteps. No danger of losing your own trail. The rest? — Buy the ones that amuse you. And the most materialistic gold, to pay for friendship, will be the purest gold. Your house is simply furnished. One fine day: you're sick of the sight of it! Midnight flit.

Love?... Over-happy lovers make a couple like a hermaphrodite monster or Siamese twin brothers. If it can't be untied, this Gordian tangle must be severed, this serpents' nest...[35]

Two parallel lines meet at infinity... I've never been able to appreciate this definition. Who will define infinity for me? — It's plain to see that I don't have a scientific mind.

Shadow boxing.

I am (the "I" is) the outcome of God multiplied by God divided by God:

$$\frac{\text{God} \times \text{God}}{\text{G O D}} = me = God$$

(What strange ways of dealing with the absolute! One can see that... etc...)

In whom to trust, Lord?

If he deceives us (whoever he is), if he makes just one mistake, we lose our faith. But if, in a thousand rummagings, I should once put my finger on God, (at the bottom of my heart and even if I tell myself not to) here I am turned prophet.

From the invisible, my lookout suddenly exalted cries: "Universe!"

But pride isn't long in falling from my hands and I give you my vote.

With you I give my word to the enemy: What a claim! It's a maniac, she sees them everywhere.

Surround and then surprise the miracle. May sulking, renunciation, fasting, serve to simplify my surroundings.

I close my eyes to put a limit on the orgy. There is too much of everything. I keep quiet. I hold my breath. I lie down, curled up, abandoning the confines of my body, I fold myself in on an imaginary center...

As a child I was already playing this game of being an invalid: It will be easier if I hop. Sharing out the cake while cutting my bit up again. If a cube doesn't fit into my construction, I withhold it. One by one I remove them all.

This is not without an ulterior motive... I shave my head, wrench out my teeth, my breasts — anything that is embarrassing or annoying to look at — stomach, ovaries, the brain, conscious and covered in cysts. When I have but one card left in my hand, just one heartbeat to notice, but to perfection, of course I will win the trick.

Post-mortem. — No. Even then, reduced to nothing, I would understand none of it. No more. Who cannot swallow it all cannot swallow the tiniest bit of it.

Anybody, faced with anything, can find something to marvel at:
(Complimenting his microscope): Universe!
(Discouraging his telescope): Atoms![36]

Tendency to push everything to the absolute, and thus: to the absurd.

Self-Love.
The death of Narcissus has always seemed totally incomprehensible to me.[37] Only one explanation seems plausible: Narcissus did not love himself. He allowed himself to be deceived by an image. He didn't know how to go beyond appearances. Had he fallen in love with the face of a nymph rather than his own, his mortal impotence would have remained the same.

But had he known how to love himself beyond the mirage, his would have been a happy fate, the epitome of living paradise, the myth of the privileged man, worthy of envy down the centuries.

That beautiful child was able to extract the infinite from his reflections, while we remain vibrations away, always the same, incapable of going any further.

O Narcissus, you could love yourself in everything: sun, your brother, even more beautiful in the weary night, who reflects a pallor on the moon which he never wearies of admiring; moon, who can only see its body in the lake where it lies stretched out until dawn; all colors scattered and each seeks out the most faithful copy of itself among the valley's multicolored columbines; honeys that the bees, your sisters, are so partial to, and where the flowers seek out their fragrance...

You were able to love yourself among wood spirits and nymphs, flattering or truthful mirrors, unconscious instruments of a separate will. And you remained apart because you would have been able, through your divinity, to isolate yourself from the universe, experience your existence, know and love yourself.

Can this Narcissus die withered, he whose self-love is fulfilled in an egoism for two, for many, for all, in the universal orgy?

Self-Love.

A hand grips a mirror — a mouth, nostrils palpitating — between swooning eyelids, the mad fixity of dilated pupils... In the brutal horizon of an electric lamp, palest yellow, mauve and green under the stars, that's it, in all modesty! what I would like to clarify in the mystery: the neo-narcissism of a practical humanity.

My picture would be of a hypocritical and sensual age where men will prefer their own contact and its silent scorn to the noisy love of others.

Would anyone think it impossible? Juxtapose morality and other loves against this picture. The silvering of mirrors thickens.

No longer absolute, but agreeably relative, the being becomes an individual. Pride becomes virtue. The body knows and absolves itself.

The myth of Narcissus is everywhere. It haunts us. It has never ceased to inspire the things that make life perfect since the fateful day when that wave without wrinkles was captured. For the invention of polished metal derives from a clear narcissian etymology.

Bronze — silver — glass: our mirrors are almost perfect. We still suffer from their vertical position; yet it's more comfortable than lying flat on your stomach on the lawn. Lazy people stretched out on their shadow gaze at themselves in the sky. But should some nuisance wrench them from their indolence, with the sound of broken glass, the reflection shatters.

Now would be the moment to fix the image in time as it is in space, to seize completed movements — surprise oneself from behind.

"Mirror," "fix," these are words that have no place here.

In fact, what troubles Narcissus the voyeur most is insufficiency, when his own gaze is interrupted.

Narcissus and Narcissus.

Marriage contract:
As stupid as a baptism. But if I have the grace not to recant, sweet revenge! Catechism, communion, confirmation, mass and everything!

Recantation:
Suicide — divorce on the grounds of incompatible moods.

Jealousy:
Caught in the act of being unfaithful to one's own temperament.

Adultery:

For some the body, for others the soul, plays the part of the lenient husband.

The parents-in-law:

Sometimes they separate us, sometimes bring us back together. But without ever having known a thing about it.

Absolute Narcissism:

Noncooperation with God. Passive resistance.

Adjourned for a week.

The man struggles in the arms of destiny:

— Not yet, Lord! I'm only ninety. Admit that it would be premature to judge my work, this first draft of body and soul.

Quiet games.

This is the torment of Tantalus.[38] But what makes Narcissus despair is not that he cannot drink himself, nor the solid, infrangible mirror-bound space,[39] the coldness that separates the glass from the image. Between him and himself, something else exists to be smashed. Always a quarter moon, never the full one. Always a partial clarity. He sees enough of his ideal for the rest of the world to disgust him — little, too little, nothing to make him happy.

A look attracts him, a mouth rebuffs him. He applies himself to the proud scrutiny of a new power and finds himself confronting the opposite of his triumph: this power is a new weakness.

40 —

What contradictions does dreaming not bring to deceitful reality? — I want this thought, I see it... Stop there, reproduce it in the
sky. I painfully sculpted this muscle; will it melt in my own heat
while I wear myself out making some other improvements, while I
still have so much to do.

Why does God force me to change faces? Why does God wreak
havoc with my deplorable qualities? Under this Penelope's tooth the
spider's thread snaps...[40] Why am I unraveled the minute I close my
eyes?

I can't answer my own questions. Maybe another time I'll place
my nets better...

III

E. D. M.

"Surely you are not claiming to
be more homosexual[41] than I?..."

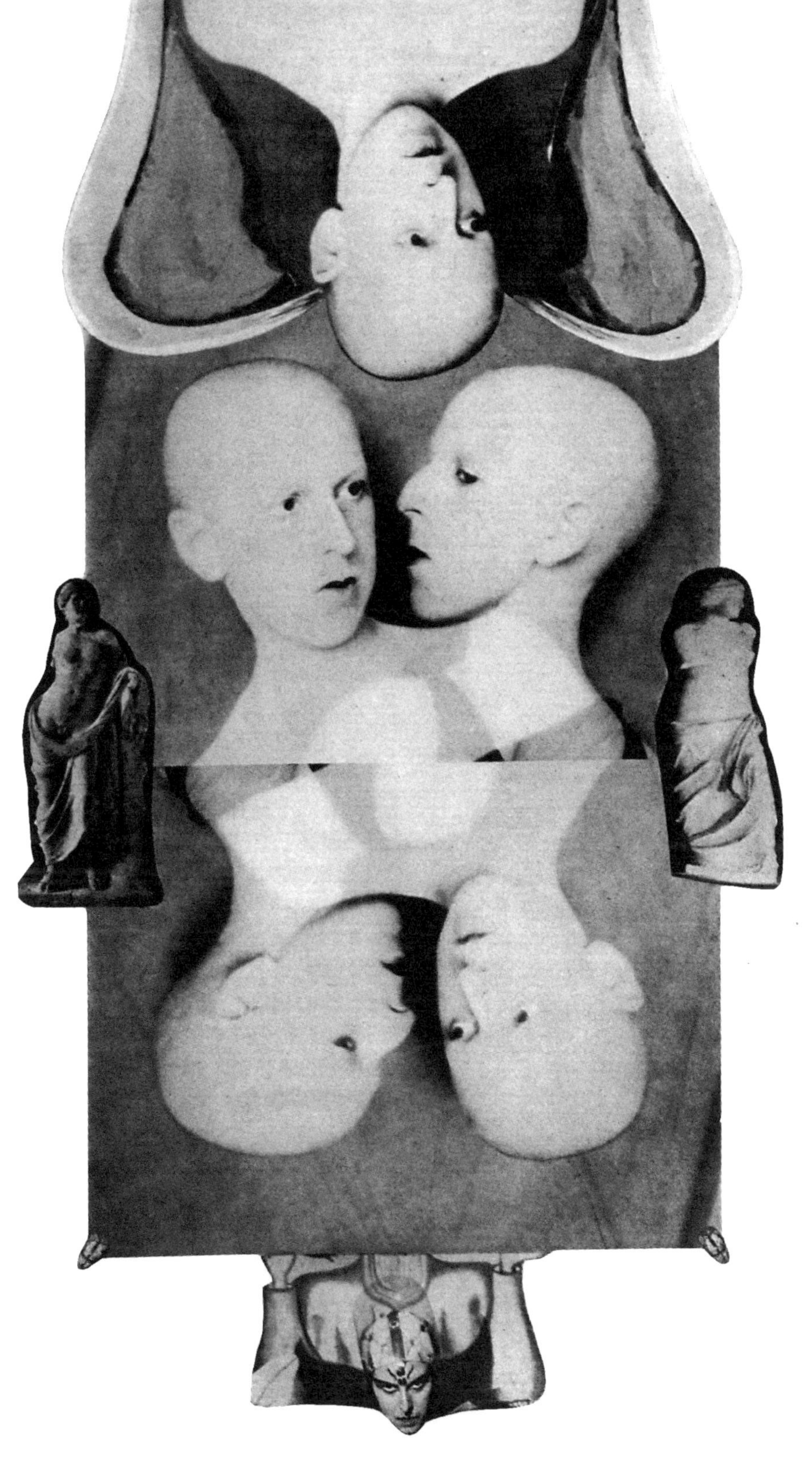

MOROSE
DELIGHTS

(about forgetting)
The curtain had been raised
five
maybe six times;
but it ended up unlifted
staying down on the Actor.

I remain alone with my prey
palpitating now, it will escape me,
alone in a blurred crowd,
which will go far away, dispersing,
poring over a problem
of insufficient gifts.

I'll try so hard to see her floating hair again
smudged in the stage set,
hairnet of stars,
delicate network of the uncombed night...

In vain
My memory swells in vain.

Beside you,
Life

(Actor)
how poor am I!
Come back,
be it in an ugly role,
deliver me from morose
remembrance,
fill my empty
eyes,
compel me to lift one more eyelid.

In vain.
My memory swells in vain,
gorged with its false treasures,
everything I pull out from there,
wilted, spineless,
is like seaweed out of the water.

It's my whole life that I pull from there,
Everything called into question
for not having known how to live so that
on the day of reckoning,
the festival day,
that today
I might have been able to prolong for an instant
this instant sunk without trace.

(about forgetting)
Certain pleasures too fresh
to produce all their flavor
need to ferment
like grape juice
and grow old

in the cellars of our memory.

From now on one will wonder
whether morose delight,
passed through the sieve of time
isn't preferable to pleasure.
It is the juice of it,
the corrupted liquid
concentrated, purified,
stronger and more lasting.

If you prefer late wine
made from sunburned grapes,
each season you will make
the vintage of your memories.
And drink them at your leisure.

(about a difficult child)
Recognize in this son
the mysterious mixture
of seed.

And when love is over,
meditate on its growing proof,
and sorrowfully rejoice.
May a downward smile
explain and deny
the bitter fold of your mouth.

Be indulgent to your son;
look after him well, this hypocrite,
beautify this talkative keepsake,

give thanks unto him:
You can make us believe in admirable love
which in the old days was never yours.

(about love)
They passed close by me
the lovers,
more loving and more pure than ever we were,
buried under a heap of caresses.

They were oblivious of my presence,
my envy, admiration or shock.
They passed close by without seeing me,
heedless, not noting my emotion.

And more than anything
their disdain was harsh delight to me.
And their unconcealed tenderness, my pleasure.

Lovers, fear nothing from me:
My jealousy wavers between you, undecided...
I resent your abstraction, that's all.

(about art)
These marble statues firm and polished
more than the best pumiced skin,
these bodies white and slim
more than the best-made Adonis,
muscles that are dear to sculptors...
— Haven't they ennobled their models?
I grant that these cold nobilities
discourage audacious lovers...

— If that! Lucien de Samosate[42] would say.

But for those who humanely seek
the evocation of a memory,
what relief these tangible images provide!

Art is the very greatest morose delight,
a sad and tender attempt to immortalize our pleasures,
to remember passing love.

(about a painful moment)
— At the time, I can assure you,
it had nothing agreeable about it;
it didn't seem to be anything at all.

Morose sensuality
matured by memory...
Just at its best for suffering.

Vocation

Does anyone have the right to be jealous of you? Which man of
our times is rich enough to possess you? Who would be permitted to
hide you away? You are too handsome, too dear, too famous! You are
a museum piece, public property.

Will anyone dare censure the Venus of Praxiteles[43] for offering
herself to everyone: naked, beguiling, immodest — indifferent?

The misunderstood beggars

Who wishes for caresses receives blows. Turn the sentence around and say with me: "It's even more shameful! It's the ultimate insult!"

These ones are asked for a little gold, or if not gold (which doesn't exist anymore), a similar product. No empty phrases: Let someone sign me a check and say no more.

They will willingly give more than they've been asked for (the superfluous in the absence of necessities): good words, bits of advice to be paid in cash...

Those ones (who are not the same ones), are asked for a little love, some "seeming-love." We'd be happy with some counterfeit coins,[44] with false smiles, a trouser button... We promise not to check their alms.

But here they are giving you a complimentary ticket, a dinner — a hundred-sou coin — instead of the dear word you expected.

Affectations.

Sodom, city of light

We say "Fire from the Sky"[45] to simplify things, like telling children they were born in a cabbage. In reality, Sodom blazed up by itself at the amorous contact between its inhabitants and the Angels of the Lord God.

That master of ceremonies, parsimonious, had only provided
one pair of them — O communism!... Speed was essential. Rub two
flints together, you'll see sparks fly! Dry wood itself (if you know
how to set about it) is inflammable.

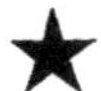

Fourth dimension

My angel is often late. I willingly wait but what is left of me
when they finally turn up?

A shout — Help! But why? Why did I call you? Tension, resistance.
I fell asleep, paralyzed. I had moved without knowing it: my crowd
had jostled me...

The angel arrives and the thing escapes me where their intervention could give us the universe or love.

Clairvoyant

Feminism is already among the fairies. Magicians will show our little boys that one can dispense with these dried-up wet nurses. And life will be no less continuous as a result nor less discontinuous.

Once upon a time there were two sorcerers whose patience was legendary. They had traced the sources of rivers and tidal currents where the fishes warmed themselves. They had lovingly observed the reproductive processes of various animals, from anemones to man. They knew how to prepare the philosophers' seed.[46]

One full moon (the moon joins the party), our two wise men brought together all of magician-kind, scattered among the peoples, for their wedding night. And having united in the traditional manner, they deposited in the cradle, which had been placed there with auspicious foresight, two little slugs: one slim, agile, green and white; the other white and green, slender, twisted. In the blink of an eye they had merged and formed just one body. It was a completely ordinary seed, a germinating, sprouting, budding grain of wheat.

And the amazed crowd witnessed a little man beginning to grow beneath their very eyes, like a plant in an unscrupulous fakir's flowerpot. With each new spurt of growth they expected that he would be missing a limb. No such thing, however. Nothing was missing, it seemed, in the composition or even the beauty of the newborn.

As soon as he stopped visibly growing — after seven seconds — the infant was chosen to be Prince (they could do no less!). And the two husbands disappeared, fearing that they might place their son in an awkward position with such a questionable and controversial paternity.

He was fourteen at the time, having lived two years a second. Already the master of bodies, he soon commanded souls. Everyone loved him — especially women. The most beautiful virgins, fairies humiliating themselves, accomplished women, all solicited him in vain. He was repulsed by the female sex; their weaknesses were all the more apparent to him since he hadn't had a mother to deposit, incubate and hatch blind love in his heart.

This is the role of women, the only one that really matters to them: to inspire breast worship in the newcomer, whoever he is: black or white, ill-formed or deformed, made of ice, of fire or cinders.

All around the Prince the crafty besotted beings whispered, claiming that in them and them alone lay the mystery without mystery, the equivalent of this world with its reason for being, the phases of the tides, the pulsation of the soil, the orgasm of the planets, everything that he still found incomprehensible due to the influence of some evil spell.

Clairvoyant only heard those words: "evil spell," and went away brooding... His birth was described as obscure. It did not befit a nobleman's dignity to know nothing of his ancestors. He set about finding them.

This was easy enough: The double androgynous seed is a mixture of unidentifiable proportions; and this mixture can produce a new body, different from those who created it, averse, hostile to any attempts at closeness. But the male seeds align themselves side by side and their alloy is a simple and stable blend.

The Prince recognized his father and mother right away — we'd better say "his parents." He complained to them about an excess of honesty which caused his senses to render everything that came near him, everything he touched, sterile.

"Do you wish for illusion, my son?" asked the less wise magician (because the other was mute). "Look at my husband, my brother: you have deeply disappointed us.

"However, I will grant you your whim. Take this ring: it contains the missing seed, the one we wanted to spare you at your birth..."

The ridiculous young lad put the engagement ring on his finger and went out into the night.

As he took his third step he saw something that made him stop, filled with wonder: "What a chaste, ideal and gracious vision! This can be nothing less than a goddess..." For we always identify as chaste the things that affect us physically.

He threw himself at her... and the sow (for it was a sow) who had no prejudices, no bias against human flesh, after a short grunt of surprise and love, gulped down this unexpected truffle of a white and monstrous variety in one go. Then, having savored it slowly, assimilated it.

IV

C. M. C.

Permit me to warn reckless young
women: seeing the trap doesn't prevent you from getting caught in it
and that doubles the pleasure.

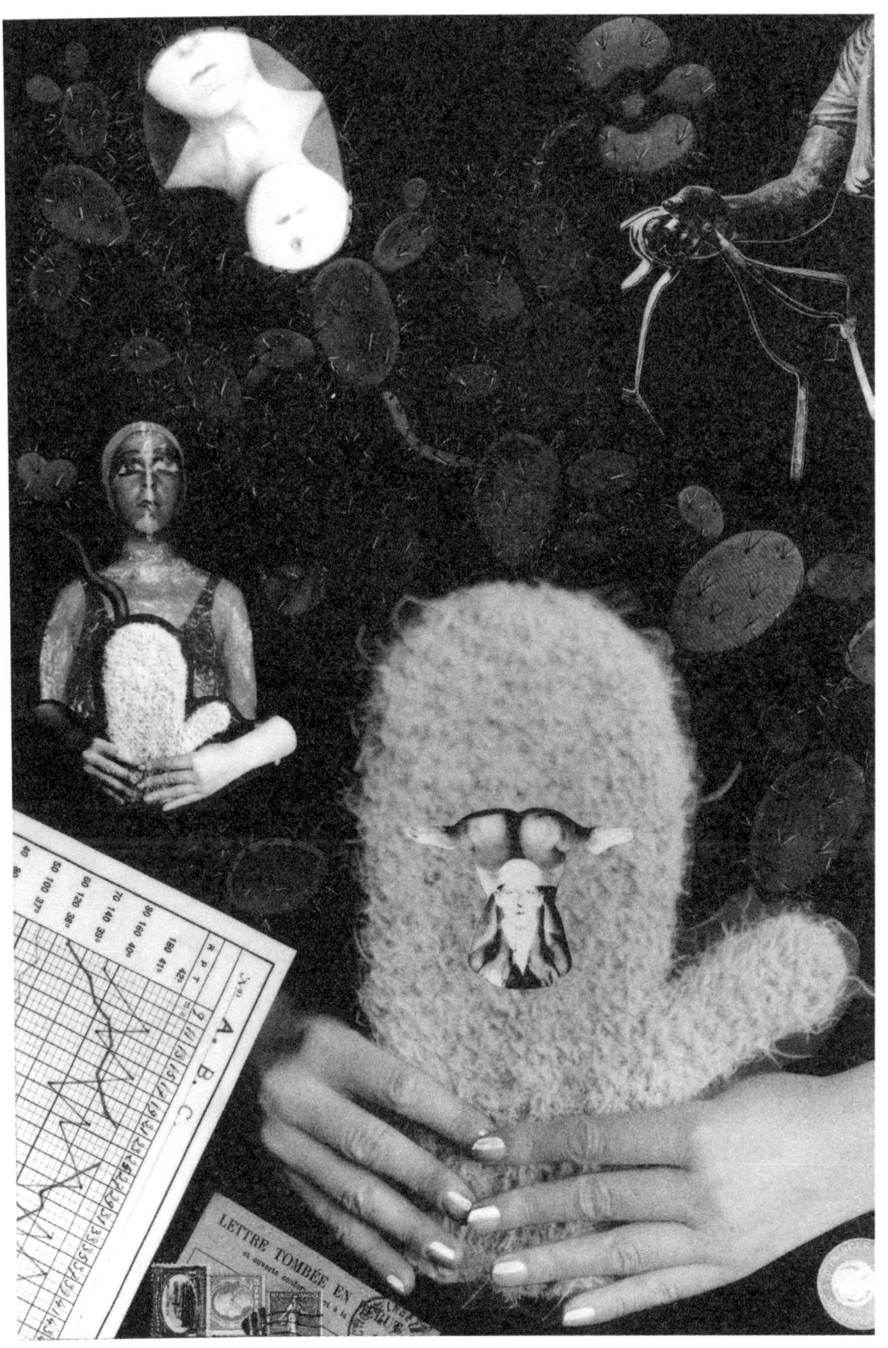

A . B . C .
LETTRE TOMBÉE EN

A U R I G E[47]

PORTRAIT

Ferocity, lasciviousness, a monstrous egotism... There are plenty of inconsistent circumstances and details; it could be toned down... but what for? We should learn to select only what is essential. Easy enthusiasms, faithful and lasting — but hardness of heart.

Redundant breasts; irregular, ineffectual teeth; eyes and hair of the blandest color; hands delicate enough but twisted, deformed. The oval head of a slave; forehead too high... or too low; a nose fashioned well enough of its type — a hideous type; the mouth, too sensual: pleasing when you're hungry but once you've eaten it makes you want to vomit; the chin hardly juts out at all; and body-wide the muscles barely sketched.

Triumphant woman!... sometimes triumphant in the face of the most appalling embarrassments, a last-minute deftness corrects a shadow, an unwise gesture — and beauty is reborn.

For in front of her mirror Aurige is touched by grace. She consents to recognize herself. And the illusion she creates for herself extends to a few others.

INSET

It is the turn of the accused to speak:

"The quest for man. That's where I've got to. But it wasn't always like that: didn't I swear eternal love to her as a child? She already had good sense back then! I remember it well (the sufferings of those times formed my memory: a painfully raw memory), very well, O precocious wisdom! — for you replied: "You are wrong... As for me, no! I can promise you nothing like that... How long? I don't know. I only know that I love you... Yes, I will get married... When? Soon, no doubt." — Admirable candor! And wasted... I was incapable of appreciating it — and that's understandable: impassioned, almost hysterical, unworthy... and far from coveting it, hating all the serenity in the world with great fervor!

"By dint of insisting I persuaded her to promise me one year — she agreed, but reluctantly. She had told me to leave that day, shut herself in her room, alone, to think deeply about such a serious decision. She came out. I was there: 'Well?' I asked (for I couldn't stop thinking about it. Nor could she, come to that). But she replied: 'Well, what?... I am going to the garden, Mother is asking for her flowers. Are you going to stay here?' Nobody gets rid of me that easily. I am stubborn: Forever, say, forever? — I am bargaining; and seeing that she's about to get angry reduce my claims: one year, say, one year? Just promise me one year, it's not such a big thing... Unable to evade me any longer, she gives me a hard look, thoughtful, serious: 'One year, so be it.' And it's as if she's giving money to a beggar she knows is only feigning poverty just so I'll leave her in peace.

"However, this promise wasn't a counterfeit coin; she had weighed it up, she intended to keep it. She did keep it generously. To her great credit, she is absolutely loyal above everything else.

"This then was the malicious genesis of our love. And here we are, nearly fifteen years later..."

PSYCHOLOGICAL PORTRAITS

No. I will only do rough sketches. When the mechanism has been completely deconstructed, the mystery remains intact. Sometimes chance hands us a little swatch of soul. We put it away in a drawer. Soon it will be impossible to match it with the piece of fabric it originally came from, now become a dress or curtain, faded, washed, often re-dyed. My comparison is still rather feeble and poor.

Nevertheless, I will take pleasure in uttering some unfair and provisional words, and say enough of them to highlight the force of illusion each carries in his glands, the force that allows him to overlook temporarily the most obvious points of conflict.

Taking it as read that man, by nature, allows his life to be governed by: fear, his sex drive, vanity, greed, compulsive lying, self-idolatry, pride — and all shades of these seven virtues — I'd like to limit myself to simply noting that in the present context Aurige represents true love, her master fear and pride, and her lover worldly vanity. Of course, at the beginning of the crisis, all three will be martyrs to their sex drives. But their familiar demons will quickly regain the upper hand.

Let us open this triptych for a moment:

A: Aurige

principal characteristics: weakness and egotism.

declared ideals: the underlying force of all things, the desire to change, to reconstruct oneself.

B: Aurige's proprietor

principal characteristic: reserve.

secret ideal: dignity.

C: the poet, Aurige's lover

principal characteristics: the need to get involved in everything, an inconsistent and easily squandered energy...

declared ideal: renunciation.

This is far too cursory. I will never define them as well as they define themselves. I'm going to ask them questions and write down their replies. That will be better; they're sure to betray themselves whatever they say.

What would you like to be?
A — More and better. My own perfection. And everyone else's into the bargain.
B — A fish in the sea, a lizard in the sun — a seal, a happy animal.
C — Buddha, a great man, a well-known dramatist, *some great poet like Swinburne or Baudelaire*, an asphodel or any other flower for they're all beautiful, a simple gentleman farmer from a very old noble line retired from the world or Sakyamuni...[48] An oriental queen, depraved and refined, whom none can resist and who harbors only scorn for all her suitors.

What would you like to do?
A — The impossible.
B — Have a very simple life, a life with nothing to do.
C — Write beautiful dramatic comedies, live in the tranquility of the fields or in the beauty of a sumptuous palace, waited on by a thousand slaves in great luxury, make a success of all my friends' lives, launch the most famous film stars, direct X's play... which all Paris will flock to see and bring in lots of money for poor Z... who is in dire need of it, make Aurige be quiet, speak instead of Jack.

What would you like to know?
A — The way to make the impossible happen, tricks of the trade, if any exist. Which path to follow — but since time is of the essence: a short cut.
B — Everything that it's perfectly useless to know. My mental curiosity knows no bounds, but I have no curiosity where my emotions are concerned, and I wish to avoid anything that might awaken them. Physically, as I've said, I'd like to have total possession of the most effective instincts for defense and protection.

C — Real occult knowledge as practiced by the initiated (I already know most of the rest of it). I'd like to know how to cure the ills of man, what diet I could follow to help my rheumatism, what antidote to give the hysterical love of our distraught mistresses... If hermaphrodites really exist, if Madame X... sleeps with men. Know how to make potions for love and immortality, the recipe for the hemlock Socrates took to die in beauty.

What distinguishes you. Which characteristics are your most obvious?

A — The dominance of my body over my desire for power, the tyrannies of its weaknesses. I am not suited to grasping objective realities, or adapting to the incessant vicissitudes of life. A slow, sluggish mind; delayed reactions. Taking pride in everything I'd like to be, in my own superlative self. Systematic deprecation of all realities, starting with my own. Shyness born of *self-consciousness*. Superstitious, but never in a traditional way; I only believe in the monsters I've created myself, I will only believe in a Messiah who will come down for the me inside me, made to measure and incomparable. Inability to imagine anything concrete, proper nouns for example. Love of abstraction, of symbols.

B — Tolerance and respect for the rights of others. A sense of responsibility. Always keeping my word, however disagreeable it might be. Disdain for everything garish, rowdy, tasteless. I am always afraid of overrating myself. Complete fear about what other people think, even the ones I most despise — at least of their overt disapproval: that has an unpleasant physical effect on me. A great indifference towards my real desires as soon as any obstacles are put in their way. A horror of taking the initiative, of anything new, risking failure. A reluctance to admit I am wrong when it comes to small matters, to details. On the whole, a modesty which seems to alarm my friends. They don't realize that deep down I never lose the sense of my secret superiority, of my goddess Reason. An active and discerning critical sensibility. A taste for debate, logic, precision, poetry, for illogicality with all its papers in order, words for words' sake. A horror of anything ridiculous.

C — A sense of theater, love of beauty, poetry, refinement, a gentleman's education, not taking offense, protection of the weak, love of animals, extravagance, courage, energy, intelligence, practical good sense, poetic imagination. Staggering speed of thought. Clairvoyance. Asceticism. Creative force.

What are your least obvious traits?
A — Courage, physical endurance, what they call strength of will, altruism, common sense — not at the point of conception but always in the execution.
B — Vanity. All the qualities that we French consider to be the perogative of Americans and Jews: brute ambition and aggressive (sometimes even defensive) artifice. And yes, to a certain extent, the instinct for preservation.
C — Egoism, vanity, skepticism, taking pleasure in destroying things, English hypocrisy, French indiscretion, stubbornness, sensuality.

What do you like about yourself?
A — My ceaseless astonishment with life. My infantile questionings. The warm feelings I have for anybody I meet, at the very first glance (as short as that is), at the first word. My refusal to judge anything without having first taken everything into consideration. My moral vacillations. My scrupulous and scandalous candor. My need for perfection.
B — This is the hardest question. I've never thought about it. I can only reply in a negative fashion: the things which could be even worse. However, to reply positively, common sense.
C — My equanimity, good education, virility, detachment from material things. A philosopher's wisdom and a poet's humane passion.

What do you least like about yourself?
A — My cowardice.
B — Everything that could make me suffer or make others suffer.
C — My fatigue, my rheumatism, my poor blood circulation, my imperfect earth-bound reasoning. My excessive forbearance, my exaggerated gentleness, my sensitivity and my limitless generosity.

What displeases you the most in general?

A — Being caught off guard, being forced to change my plans, replying without preparation, writing with no crossings-out, being seen without makeup, even if that makeup gives me an ugly hue, suffering from badly strung nerves. That was the reply my body just gave. — From the point of view of sensitivity, I will reply: human beings. Everything about them that seems to me superficial, conventional, unjust, greedy, unreasonable, secondhand. Human cruelty. But my guess is that that's not so much about loathing as fear. I always identify with the victims. — I find it difficult to reply on the intellectual level, all I can say is: It displeases me, privately, to catch myself in the wrong even if over a trifle. I instantly lose confidence in the entire universe. All in all, it's still a passionate approach.

B — Vulgarity, folly, mental weakness, ugliness, lack of self-control. And everything that affects the senses disagreeably.

C — Ugliness, malice, pretentiousness, stupidity, Anglo-Saxon idleness, Breton tyranny and stubbornness, scenes, anger, ingratitude, complacency and conceit. The cruelty of man towards flies and horses.

What pleases you?

A — For my body: calmness, silence, darkness, sunshine, swimming in the sea at dawn (in summer), the light intoxication derived from several days' fasting. For my passions: human beings, their strength, their health, their balance; but also beautiful imbalances and lovely weaknesses. Recognizing myself in them, idealized by a flesh more appealing than my own. And then: everything that gives me a strong impression of something new yet easily assimilated.

B — Sleep, dreams, the sea, sunshine, gaiety, sport, books, paintings, silence, contemplation (daydreaming). Protecting and maybe tyrannizing a little. Animals, children. Ideas.

C — Animals, innocent trees, flowers, women who are beautiful, elegant, depraved, supremely indifferent and detached, Nature, Sakyamuni and the Art of the Poet.

What do you hope for?

A — The unknown, a hope previously unacknowledged. The miracle that is yet to come.

B — The past. The repetition of the past until death. I mean that's the happiest that I can imagine. I expect nothing from the future. Nothing except ordinariness. Or maybe the atmosphere of dreams, life becoming easy. Or eternal sleep with or without dreams.

C — Nirvana.

What do you fear?

A — The unknown. That I would give up on myself at the same time as my master succeeded in intervening to conceal my emptinesses, my stupid pastimes, my shortcomings from me. Feeling that I am not attaining my true level, low as it already is. Unbearable physical suffering.

B — Suffering.

C — The past beginning all over again.

Happiest moments of your life?

A — Dreaming. Imagining myself to be different from how I am. Playing my preferred role.

B — Indifference. Sleep. Dreams. Or the simple, purely physical life.

C — That's really indiscreet! — and not very interesting.

The most unhappy?

A — Physical, emotional and intellectual suffering. I wouldn't know how to decide which is the worst.

B — When other people annoy me. When Aurige is in a bad mood. Worries about the future, indecision, insomnia.

C — When I see people who have loved me dying.

Why are you afraid to suddenly die, at this precise moment?

A — My unfinished sentence left at the planning stage. How restful! My distress isn't based on when but how I will have to chuck it all in. And there, I confess, the cowardice of this body, of this bitch body, terrifies me.

B — I am not afraid.

C — Certainly not, quite the opposite. Stupid question!

Why do you prefer yourself to all others?

A — Because this person is the only one I can use to prefer everyone else. She is the nearest thing to me, the implement I have at hand. Because I feel, because I am, because I cannot do otherwise.

B — But that's not the case. If I sometimes happen to show some kind of preference for myself, it's through absentmindedness. Aurige is always one step ahead of me. In my mind, I judge lots of others to be preferable to us.

C — So it's insults now is it? Prefer myself! The first *gentleman* who comes along will give you an appropriate answer.

EXPLANATIONS

B — Listen Aurige! If you love him, leave me. I don't want you to but I'll get over it... Don't start thinking you're indispensable.

A — (How to reply to that?)... I don't love him enough to leave you...

B — Well, Aurige, since it's me you love after all, you have to be honest and stop lying.

A — (How to reply to that?)... I don't wish to lie. It's him, it's you who compels me to do it. I certainly don't love him, but I am afraid that I don't love you either... not enough to be "honest." (Does he really exist?... no, no! but it's more a question of whether it's really necessary to be "honest"?)

C — Stay with your master, Aurige, but sleep with me. He'll look after you better than I ever could... (translate as: I will never take the trouble to do so) — and I'll be there for Art, Dreams, Love... You must just promise me this — when you make love with your master, I am always aware of it, you know that — promise to love only me, to sleep only with me...

A — (At least I can reply to that!)... But why, why? Since I feel I am perfectly capable of sleeping with both of you.

LETTERS FROM AURIGE TO THE POET

> Dead letter: You shall not
> take the name of love in vain.

How short these hours were!... How did I get the sad courage to leave when you were letting me stay? Now it all seems superhuman to me — and so stupid! Should I have waited to be chased away... or nearly...

I am consoling myself (badly) by thinking that I took the only chance for having you miss me...

What! With all those wonderful beings around you... you'd have had time to think of me! And me so small... *It's a mistake, but do still make it.* Continue to make this sweet mistake with me.

... and so, O treasured memory, will you perhaps come to be born again in my life? For our thoughts and deeds are constantly born again to counteract their incessant deaths. Poet, have you thought of this?

... and the ill-disciplined pupil can offer you only a little of her madness in exchange, and you have no more use for that than she has for your rationality.

Despite my determined friendship, and though I am (O shame!) precisely of that vulgar type *"who must lay heavy hands on life,"* I can detach myself from you. I have endured so many sacrifices in my life! I'm used to it. So I will joyfully accept all that you impose on me. But — *despite the appeal to my beloved Plato* — (ah!... you already know the weak spots in my mind and you take advantage of them!), don't hope to lead me into choosing renunciation. This season it runs contrary to my mood.

On the other hand, I cannot bring myself to "find the actions of the flesh ridiculous" — some actions, above all the most useless ones, actually seem beautiful to me, like an art form, due to their vanity, their perfect sterility. — Or else I'll condemn all actions, even those of the mind... and absolute Stupidity — the kind that can neither grow nor perish, the most unwavering Error, the most deep-rooted, will be my idol... Come on, Poet! Don't look at me like that: I'm not as debauched as I try to appear. I'm making myself out to be a bad person, that's all.

We went into the unfriendly town today; — it seemed strangely changed to me. Melancholy memories of our recent walks ambushed me at every turn in the street, and I thought I saw you walking a few steps ahead of me...

Don't get bored. It's bad for your health. Do anything crazy you can think of instead!...

I am desperately hungry for all kinds of drugs. It's this damned lust obviously. My Master, so generous with freedom in some circumstances, is suggesting he buys me enough alcohol to get really drunk. No, thank you! It's too brutal for me...
But...
(He allows me this reading: a pleasing tyrant all in all!)
You have to comfort yourself in whatever way you can.

— Woman? Oh, yes! — Alas, who are you saying it to! Poet, cruel. But you write me things so wonderfully compensatory that you almost reconcile me with myself. Me! — the very modest Narcissus. I'm going to explain my *self-love* to you... It's fake. Pure stoicism, maybe some pride... In reality, I have a huge need for other people.

... And I am ready slyly to break all my promises — provided that you would accept my soul, impervious to all scruples as it is, without contempt, or my rebellious body, or even one and the other... A body is easy to refuse, but a resolute soul!...

Braving even your contempt, my soul is devoted to you, Poet! — and you can do nothing about it...

I express myself very, very badly. There are sentences that are not made to be understood but felt, rather. What good would it do to say: "I love you"? I only wish to be able to think it very forcefully, near you, in the silence...

There is a being in the world whom I do not want to deceive at any price — and that being is you.

I would slander myself rather than try to seduce you with a simulated beauty. So, despite my self-love (intermittent fever, I assure you), I am aware of my faults, my intellectual defects and my physical flaws. I don't want you to be unaware of them either. It was out of candor, and not to shock you, that I came into your room naked yesterday.

This morning I got out my red notebook, and I tried to reconstruct in great detail every happy, incomplete yet perfect moment that I owe to you — O my friend! Alas! I am utterly alarmed by the poverty, the painful omissions of my corrupted memory (ah! I am truly punished!). Even the sequence of these moments escapes me (O elusive recollections)... But if analysis is no longer possible I still have — through my present suffering — a certain synthesis of past happiness with which to counter this gloomy day.

And I am living from this impetus, like a machine which keeps running even though its motor has stopped...

I persist more than I exist — at the mercy of your incisive writing or condemned by your resilient silence. (I don't really believe this, you know. You won't condemn me. I trust you.) But if you

measure out hope too parsimoniously – take care: in a flash of rebel-
liousness or vigor, I'll take a whole armful of my memories and hurl
them ahead. Then I'll turn toward winter where these memories will
be robust hopes. I'll be brave again – brave enough to overcome any
scruples... I'm talking about yours and not mine.

Excuse this rambling and growl at me, please, my dear. That's
probably why I am writing. My only desire now is to hear your voice,
whatever it has to say to me. Write to me.

I discovered within my pride the philosopher's stone of love.
With it, I can perform the transmutation of joys: from signs, I'll
make sounds; from sounds, I'll make perfumes; from perfumes, I'll
make kisses; from kisses, I'll obtain caresses... It's obvious that I
have this power — but do carry on as though it were nothing!...

I am resigned to following these secret paths, and, if I can, I'll
push you onto them: You must live, dear! — To me that means to
love you freely. — And would freedom exist in lies? Of course: that's
where it belongs. For centuries it has had no other dwelling. Am I
cynical? No: on the contrary, love has rejuvenated me. Often this
love was innocent to the point of clumsiness. I don't think this is its
only charm, and I regret it — my only regret!

However, the prospect of staying at..., what a dangerous hope.
— Dangerous! If it were to be disappointed. While I wait, the Master
comforts me with a kindness — alas! so badly rewarded: I must be
unbearable!

... and I could do with the soothing sea, to be calm in a way that
mustn't be confused with oblivion for that would be contrary to my
desire — and totally impracticable.

Where did I leave my beautiful indifference? The inadequacy of
that egotism of which I was so proud is the basis of imbalance.
Suppressing it completely would be as good — but then it has to be
retrieved in its entirety.

Anyway, where you are concerned, I can't take back any of my immense tenderness nor would I wish to — even if it were to make me suffer much graver torments. For I would love them.

"It occurs to you that perhaps (!) I may be troubled to know you ill"?... By Jove!... and there's no need to have a tender heart for this! I'm not too sure about mine — all in all more bad than good — but I feel utterly distraught, so powerless to ease your sorrow, incurably distanced from you! — And what would I do if I were close? If not annoy you: I scarcely know how to care for the ones I love!...

You must know how great my anguish is and how great it will continue to be until — soon, ah, soon! — I am assured of your complete recovery...

I would so much have wished to come to... if not to cure your ills, at least to try to distract you from them...

My one and only

Yes, you are unique, my little god (everyone is one, of course, but you more so than anyone else)...

You are unique and I love you, and our friendship — harsh necessity finally opens these eyes to what you fruitlessly tried for so long to show me — can become an extraordinary joy, long-lasting and unchanging, purified by the tears that sully it...

I shamefully pleaded my very bad case — and lost the trial: the Master always offers me the same harsh alternative — *the golden cage* (big enough at the end of the day) — or the universe which frightens me.

Continuing with my indecision, the horrifying childishness of my denial, brings too many sorrows, risks too many disasters!... And I've made my choice.

My values are all wrong for this life — start everything again!...

You must believe me: With you I was in the wrong, I was reckless, maybe even worse... but always loyal. And whenever I dragged you off with me, as I often did, I still doubted, despite all the proof, that men such as my Master, such as you, could exist: honest, certainly more passionate than me, repelled by the idea of sharing — so different from me, I am so demanding, debauched — abnormal. I suppose I finally have to admit it!

You are young — ah! so young and so handsome! — and you have many more very desirable conquests ahead, you will inspire pure passions in beings more worthy of you than I. I hope for this with all my heart, I who love you with a selfishness bleached by so many tears...

But maybe you will retain a simple, sure and deep friendship for me (is that too ambitious?)... I'm not jealous — at least some virtues emerge from my vices.

Don't pity me either. My lot will be the most desirable one: I have told you that I felt compelled to deify whatever I love. You replied that, if love comes true, the game becomes dangerous. From now on I will be protected from danger — and will be able to get drunk on adoration, *my one and only God!*

You see where I am: the return of egoism. My excuse, that I suffered so much during those tormented days, could do nothing but aggravate your distress. I take it back. You will forgive me for approaching you with absolutely no excuse.

Yes, I honestly (!) believed that we down here could have and hold anything we loved and desired so long as they were consenting!

But I am alone in having such thoughts. I alone am to blame. Say it, I beg you, shout it — that you have to be left in peace! Everyone should know it...

Write to me that you understand, that you forgive, that you forget, that you will be happy — already nearly cured. Don't worry about me: I am used to seeing my dreams pass me by as I drop my weak oriental arms back down to my sides...

... and why not here?

I don't know which God I am offering these futile prayers to. The Gods are indulgent but I do not believe they can answer our cries. They can scarcely maintain their own happiness! All Gods manage to give the impression that they suffer more and better than men. Therein lies their superiority.

This land is always the same: extraordinarily beautiful. But, this year, I find its beauty cold and admire it without loving it. Yet another impotent god!

Every day seems to me to take a long time to live — the evening so much preferable to the morning! (except for insomnia).

I also take great pleasure in chatting with you, listening to you above all, and always will — O wise voice of the Poet! — and telling you today about my monotonous joys and the strange anxiety which make the yet unlived days of this month (overconfident, no doubt) into moments as precious as if they were already memories — mixing the vague with the defined. Too much insecurity also: I feel myself changing minute by minute, and this together with impatience and regret. — Is the pneumatic clock aware of its tickings? Is it disturbed by its inability to slow them down or speed them up as it pleases?...

... sentences nor music. But a higher rhythm possesses me. The fresh air, the clear sea, sky without blemish — a commensurate fatigue, a well-apportioned rest...

Only a very strong attraction will take me from this land of heartfelt gaiety.[49] It's a stronger love than one feels for a homeland — this is the place where I became conscious of myself, where I started to imagine that I was thinking! Where I loved myself for the very first time.

I'm exaggerating!

Write me letters like only you know how to: living, moving, the illusion of your presence — but not like the last one which nearly made me cry... oh! only out of rage against you!

And you have no excuse: for the same words that betray me are obedient to you, and submissive...

But: I love you, and I defy you to turn this phrase against me.

"To Live in Truth and Beauty"...? An irregular wave knocks me over, leaves on my lips a trace of bitter spume. Beauty? A look half glimpsed, palpitating eyelids. I covet it, certainly, but how to attain it? Imperfect as I am, will I dare insist that it never leaves me, never tires of me?

As for "Truth," shall I confess it to you? I don't care about it in the least. I'm not looking for it: I run away from it. And I consider this to be my true duty.

These last weeks you must have, or at least you could have, been thinking badly of my friendship, if not about me myself...

I haven't written to you for a long time, I didn't reply to your last letter, affectionate as it was and full of good advice — which naturally I won't take! Alas! Weak people only ever do things their own way. They're not wondering which intellectual regime — or rather moral, don't you think? — the artist should follow in order to produce (with some "*coaxing*") a tiny little minor talent...

They live out their fantasies, destroy themselves at will, and are only creative when they feel like it... Ever violated in vain by "Truth" (with its cortege of bestializing sorrows or pleasures without dreams), but conscious of their weakness, they rigorously avoid all sacrifice offered to the heavy machine of glory that would crush them — so out of proportion with these victims, in short, so ridiculous!

They are passionate about happiness; they're obsessed with it. Happiness so difficult for them, themselves so difficult, that they will have no hesitation in burning everything that could possibly nourish their idol. The fragile yet unbreakable joy of children has seduced them. They'll be deliberately "puerile" and keep their maturity at bay unto death if they can.

If I spoke to you about art and untruths, dear incorrigible Poet (for it is the poet who revolts and declares Beauty and the "Truth," inseparable — unsociable would perhaps be more appropriate — something the philosopher could never do), if I spoke to you about art, understand that I was speaking about life — life that I call art, no doubt (without too much modesty) to give it some kind of value. I don't give a damn about literature, just like you don't give a damn about...

Don't start believing, because of this conversation which I find most agreeable... It's possible to have different opinions about the value of "Truth" and still be the best friends in the world.

... you answer ironically, and I wound myself in turn. It would be so simple to chat (or so it seems to me): observing on your dear face the reflection of a tactless word, taking it back in time, monitoring the interpretation of sentences, chastising the obscure ones, the guilty ones... Soon, maybe?

You'll have to try to convert me to "Truth." I only ask to listen to you, for you will have some admirable Poet's arguments, I am sure. And even if I don't listen to you properly, at least I'll seem as though I am — and I'll be looking at you! Who knows? Several have been converted to less...

You have the knack of making me act without thinking, saying things that my lips disapprove of — so that I am always surprised by myself.

No one else in the world gets so much out of me.

... And otherwise the sun, the sea, love, occupy my body and soul — or to put it more modestly: my mind. No doubt I don't possess much of a soul...

You're mistaken: I was twenty-seven last October.

FROM THE POET TO AURIGE

The house awaits you and the poet too. Come in three days time. You'll have every delicacy, every luxury. I've got cushions ready for you, and sorbets. Bathwater perfumed with a spray of orchids will refresh your Adonis-like body...

Don't deny it: I know everything you think... O God! It's awful being so intelligent!

This letter is the hardest I've ever had to write, for I see quite clearly that you don't understand me in the least, you have never understood me, and in all probability, you never will understand me, alas!...

I believed you to be sincere and loyal. Alas! I believed you to have a great deal of courage and talent too! That said, one needs the self-control of a Socrates not to get angry...

The most lovely women of Paris send me roses for the New Year, but you decide to send thorns. It seems to me that's in very bad taste!

I am sending your letter back unread (I can tell just by looking at it that it's written with venom), I'm not even going to read it — for the very good reason that to do so would be extremely disagreeable for me. Furthermore, I do not consider you competent in poetic matters — does anyone else?

I bear you no ill whatsoever, but don't congratulate yourself on that score: it's simply that I consider your behavior utterly childish, unworthy of your twenty-six years and of absolutely no importance.

Through my relations with other people and thanks to their approbation, thanks to their perfectly correct opinion of my worth, I have acquired an inviolable self-esteem that your total lack of esteem and respect for me could never hope to diminish.

When something displeases us, it's a simple matter to keep quiet — as I have done every time you displeased me. People of good breeding and education are well aware that this is how to behave. But I think every little Narcissus can only admire himself; yet he lets his own beauty down when he barks at others. The Original one was not interested in other people...

You really have gone too far. Perhaps I am to blame for having allowed you to insult me once too often?...

You will find below a remarkable axiom that I have composed:

"Criticism is easy but Art is hard."[50] You would do well to meditate on it. Love and Life, of which Art and Genius are the most beautiful fruits, will only ever be known by hearts that are free of your intolerable cynicism, by those whom the alchemy of Truth has designated for the Sublime Initiation.

You should concern yourself with writing a masterpiece of your own — a work of Beauty!

And never forget: Silence is Golden!

[Two months later.]

The house awaits you and the poet too. Come, here you will find rest, every delicacy, the most lovely women in all Paris and the most handsome boys of Grecian antiquity. With my own hands I have prepared for you... etc...

THEIR CONCLUSIONS

C — Aurige offered herself — and I refused her. I am the most virtuous among men!

B — The poet courted her, but Aurige preferred me. I am the happiest among men!

A — The poet is a vain peacock and impotent; my Master is brutal and clumsy — I am truly miserable!... But so many others are adorable, so many others!... I haven't said my last.

IN THE MARGIN

Change of balance.

I have given freely of my soul (prostituted her would be a better word). Nevertheless, I love you with her virgin force. But the soul has taken the name of love in vain so often that now she's ashamed and is hiding. Like the shepherd boy in the fable, she cried "Wolf!" too often and nowadays, I fear, you won't believe her.

Like all her little sisters, this soul is unfaithful — a light seed that gets tangled in your hair but the slightest movement frees her onto the compass rose, sweeps her away and up to the sky, drives her toward the flowers of the forest, toward bouquets of flowers, toward new faces... innocently distracted (let's admit it), being distracted even for an instant is too much.

Oblivious and childish, this soul is unworthy.

He,[51] my body, is pure (almost pure). He would be devoted to you, and his heavy weight could restrain the crazy prisoner. "The flesh is faithful..." — You understood all this so well, so why? Why don't you want to?

— Don't thank me, it's nothing.

Tricks

When you've dropped your love on your way somewhere, carefully retrace your unlucky steps back toward the past. Just one crossing-out and you set off again down another path. (Bah! why not the same one?)

The way to make someone happily hand over most of his privileges: take his most precious things from him.

On the burnt plain the magicians bound me with the coiled resistance of long supple grasses. I can breathe and sleep, dream, pray and even tend to the salvation of my soul. If I choose to continue living according to my carnal nature, the indulgent magicians will bring both fruits and women to my vanquished arms, to my reclining body, to my mouth.

A belated butterfly, something shining from its ephemeral flight has put a glimmer of madness in my eyes — a glimmer of hope.

Sweet naughty child, you met my eyes, you slid your penknife between my teeth; then, exploiting my gratitude, you forbade me to make use of it:

"Free yourself little by little," you told me kindly.

I worked through long inclement nights to free just one shoulder, the sweat on my weary brow scarcely cooled by the wind's short gusts. My right hand is completely numb as a result, as if it were dead.

And from flower to flower, along the horizon of trees, my beautiful butterfly (fake mayfly, most probably eternal) finally liberated from my desire will disappear from view — while a last summer sun, burning, faded, falls like a dead leaf.

Then you return, you contemplate my tears — and you reproach me sweetly.

"You should have cut yourself free from your bindings! Alas, it's too late now..."

Temptation.

"Don't forget that you have damned yourself once and for all." — a little more, a little less... — "Not even. There are no degrees of evil. One hits the bottom at once, and you feel it." I believe I am in hell, therefore I am.

Eve: Good, evil, nothing but complications! I'm not hungry for an apple. I'm hungry for your skin.

PRISONER OF THE WORD

One is blonde, but beautiful the other:
    Choose! Decide!
Leave them to their fun together
    Elsewhere. — Hide!

The lad is handsome, the girl's a beauty:
    Choose! Decide!
Betroth them both to loves' own cruelty:
    Suffer, die.

The sky is white and beautiful the earth:
    Choose! Decide!
Accept your mortal values' worth
    Whither flee? — Whither hide?

No distance between earth and sky
Nothing we can measure it by
Between my own shadow and me.
Let's leave the sleepwalker hush-a-bye
    At the edge of the roof.
    Sleep...

Who wouldn't awaken if he could!

Choose?

Choose while sleeping. Choose in vain.[52]

Attitudes.

Where relationships between people, ideas, organs are concerned, nearly the whole sequence depends on the first contact, the first fortuitous word.

You could imagine two conversations, two lives, two philosophies, divergent in every aspect, contradictory as it were, just by changing the first appearance on stage, the way the subject is first broached, the opening gambit of the game.

Human body.

It should be stuck upside down in a vase so that it arranges itself elegantly, so that it blooms, so that it has four branches, four flowers and the bulb is hidden.

Precedents

I was walking toward the sea and suddenly stumbled... my knees in the foam, a child (it's actually me) falters and laughs with fright. He contemplates the great mass of waves so much bigger than him, their strength beyond comparison with his own. They pit themselves against each other, outdo each other, cheat, stand on tiptoes, taking advantage of the unevenness of the shore, competing for height and speed with no sense of fairness. They climb on each others' shoulders, trampling the bodies of the fallen. They growl with a hollow sound, reveal their firm teeth and seize the child by the back of his knees. Panting with rage, they suddenly appear to be calm, the supreme ruse, and slyly start scooping the sand from beneath his feet... He works his lip in salutary scorn. Alas!

The poor child has aged a whole year. Shouldn't he be shielded from an oft-repeated spectacle that is becoming indecent? For now he watches his brutish big sisters with a new curiosity as they mount each other like animals, loveless and cruelly savage. In the eyes of the amazed child, the seascape (undeniably chaste) now displays an image of rutting that his adolescent body suddenly craves. It's too late to conceal the spectacle from him — and in any case what good would it do? For him, from this moment, any emptiness would be peopled by orgies.

I have just heard my laugh which has scarcely changed and I understood that faced with the sea, with love, with all the forces of the elements (we so willingly surrender!) age, sex, even individuality cease to be relevant — that maybe separation of souls and bodies that seek to unite is not possible.

Awkward moments

Privileged, until recently I had no sense of sin. But (there's no getting away with it!) other people eagerly undertake to give me false scruples and teach me at least the appearance of remorse — a simulation that makes me feel grotesque.

Out of love for whomever life has thrown at us, we alter our-selves to such an extent that if the ideal one ever came along, we'd be incompatible.

Hadn't I addressed the letters that my Master alone understood, that seemed to be written for him, to the other?

How can I describe my embarrassment? He was utterly seduced by them.

Both of you were tugging at me. It's I who am surplus to requirements: sort yourselves out.

Puffing up the indifference of my empty breast, I started to sing some much-loved song, preferring to evade the surveillance of these two violent beings, whose presence is overly indiscreet, overly simultaneous, with a handsome absent man (memory without jealousy).

You suffer from his rights (from my privileges rather more than from his tyranny).

You suffer from his desire — and maybe from mine more than anything...

Between the two, myself, too willing to share, alas! What should I do? I know how to lie, for God's sake! and don't know to dissemble.

You are tactless enough to control yourself better than me, to leave me to compromise myself alone.

And it's that, isn't it my friend, that saddens you the most.

Killing a perfectly good friendship because of a love without beauty or vitality — and which didn't even lead anywhere! Such is my folly and my punishment.

Premature Autumn

The ardor of an impassioned summer had burnt the leaves before the season of their falling.

In our love, before its fulfillment, so many dried-up feelings fall already.

Yet the sun shines undiminished.

We were finally going to love each other, there, in the clearing.

But our bed of vegetation cried out under the weight of our two bodies. And we fled the danger:

Alas! Too many dead leaves.

Bitternesses

The sea, unique lover with ever open arms.

How easy it is from afar! Peopling the empty seascape with longed-for sails, with lands and treasures.

One becomes accustomed to successive disappointments, and as if the horizon narrowed around the traveller, it is fitting that he should be alone in the middle of the ocean.

Where love is concerned, it's up close that illusion corrupts our senses.

In direct proportion to the distance he puts between himself and his beloved, the lover's thoughts circle an imaginary love, getting smaller and smaller — reach the center at last, stand still.

And his thoughts see that there is nothing, that they were moving around a void, that they exist alone.

Isn't all frustrated pleasure pointless?...
— In any case, far too literary for my taste!

By losing one's illusions about life in general, one regains respect for one's own destiny, for one's very first disillusions.

Doing the same thing, saying the same words with the other, in a spirit of penitence, and for impure pleasure, secretly, to revive my sin.

All in all, the equivalent of a flagellation — this questionable good and evil.

Let each benefit from it as he may.

— Is love really anything other than exalted suffering?

Jealousy sleeps at the moment when love should have most doubts: during an embrace.

God: It really is too stupid!
This time I completely give up.

My body frequently humiliated my thought, my body badly constructed, full of graceless mutinies. My thought took revenge by way of mirrors which it sought out, lovesick, sadistic — always torturing itself in them.

My thought brings the recalcitrant body to face its reflection and makes it stay there; my thought affects surprise and pretends not to recognize the body at first; then criticizes it and judges it — judges the body unworthy of it — finally sending it to sleep like a guard so that it can escape this sordid prison. Sometimes it gets caught in the trap if it has to clink glasses and drink something narcotic together.

One evening, thanks to some sort of disguise, I crossed the threshold unnoticed by the demon who stunned passing dreams with bludgeon blows...

I crossed, drunk and nearly reeling from all the new, extraordinarily harmonious sensations, a beach of soft sand, the color of wing powder, no sooner touched than tarnished. I had the first misfortune when I turned and lowered my head. (Yet I had told myself that it's an immortal sin to look at your own footprints!) I couldn't find the shape of my own steps anymore. Their distinct traces were now like a stranger's, and the oblique line of toes, elongated by the

deformed big toe which had so exasperated me that same morning,
was nowhere to be seen.

Mad with a regrettable curiosity, and guided by my customary
passion, I peered at the reflections in the wet sand:

A well suddenly opened and I saw myself at the bottom.

(O this care for precision! Shouldn't we live in the lie, never
checking things — even if it were an illusion? Haven't I said it and repeated it myself?) Anyway, I saw myself and looked at myself:

And the horror of the unknown took hold of me, horror of this
mysterious, much-coveted beauty which, it seemed to me, had poun-
ced on my soul like a bird of prey, brought it to its nest, enveloped it
entirely and devoured it...

I had a presentiment of disaster...

If I thought only of the ugly flaws of my despised body, quickly
and with enough force, I still could, for certain! halt the collapse of
the known universe.

Alas! My thoughts were not strong enough...

Almost despairing, I made the effort of Atlas, the motion of
his superhuman vault (only, in my case, I carried the world on my
humped back.)

I woke up.

And touching each of my deformed, hideous and hateful limbs, I
declared myself safe and well.

Hymn

All sweetness, son of omnipotence, all tenderness, God of children — ah! that I were complicit in your goodness.

O too merciful, I suffer because I wasn't able to share your punishment, I suffer even more that I have no reason to hope that I will
see you here again, man among men.

(O in all eternity couldn't you have waited two thousand years to come to save my brothers?)

But if we eventually become worthy of your redemption, won't you come down among us, a fitting reward, sacrificing your joy for us instead of your pain?

Weaknesses

I am faithful to pain alone — and that very much despite myself.

Poet, and arranges himself a creative derangement of the emotions, a methodical derangement.[53] Poet? Sick man who goes on a diet.

If it's not about me, why should I care?

I endorse it. For and against. And will wash my hands in my own blood.

May others murder you systematically, link by link, heart after heart, caterpillar! And may others avenge you.

I am in the fist and in the wound; I recognize myself here, there and everywhere. I will not intervene.

No blinkers, that's ignoble. And without blinkers I cannot write, at least not otherwise than I have always done. Like a skittish horse. And if "write" should be replaced with any other verb of action, my sentence loses none of its assurance.

A new verb, a new object — and the same subject. Always the same chain of complaints.

With the least effort I can distinguish three cowards within. One forsakes me, or the other two, or all three at the same time: "I don't know." "I don't want anything to do with it." "I'm ill."

I even evade my own evasion: "Too late. — Tomorrow." And go back to sleep.

Return to harbor

You got agitated by some of my absurdities (sometimes the most useless ones), agitated in a haphazard way without any particular discernment.

You reproached me for having got up in the middle of the night to watch a train go by (yes, like cows do!), probably insignificant but I imbued it with a dear presence... You condemned certain looks (which you alone were capable of seeing), God knows which of my acquaintances, and my idolatry (that's divine vengeance), and my verbal extravagance (shameful, literary). I acknowledged this any-way, you are right; but it's my ambition to live according to truths other than the literal truth. A simple accumulator which takes the electricity it requires wherever there is an available current — that's what I am. That's what I have to be. I am marvelously indifferent to my passions (interchangeable according to the most suitable occasion so as to appear voluntary). The spectacular result of them on my soul engages me beyond all scruples.

Looks, acquaintances, idolatry, lies, you make me see them as infantile, and I would resent you for having betrayed all my puerilities if it weren't perhaps the only way for me to rid myself of them, to liberate myself from slavery, my Master.

But understand for one moment what it is that always distinguishes you from others: They — my reasons for living — are but a pretext; you are one of them, sometimes it's like that. But sometimes too you are what they will never be, my reason for being.

Come on, let's exaggerate a little: Them — life. You — death. You know very well which I prefer and who, fatally, prevails.

V

M. R. M.

I played with words, these colors without danger. Forgiveness but forgiveness for something else. And it's so serious, so total that I hardly dare... Everyday life, this abomination! I exist and that comprises everything. Forgive me for existing.

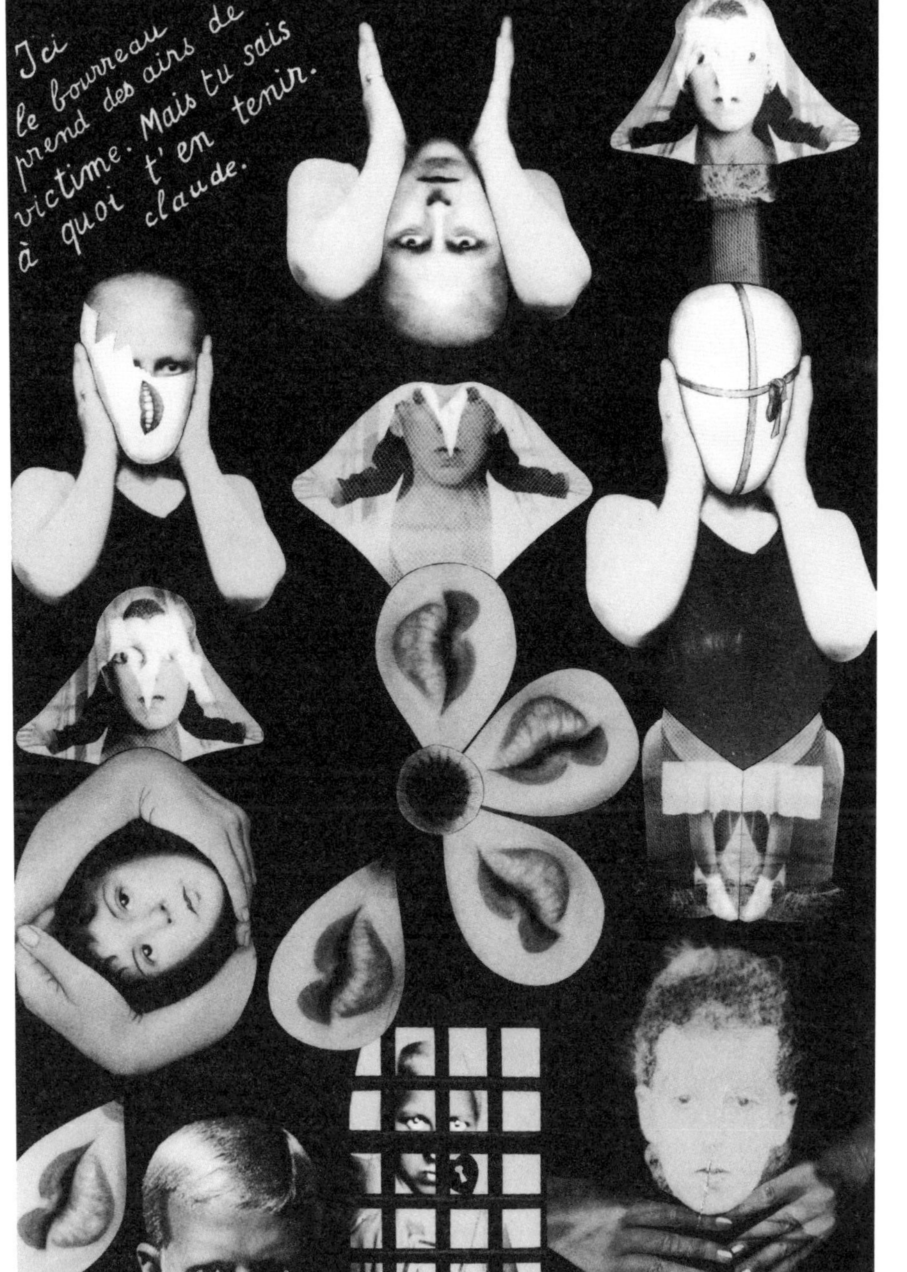

Ici
le bourreau de
prend des airs de
victime. Mais tu sais
à quoi t'en tenir.
claude.

Portrait of Mlle X

(photo if possible...)

Some strands of barbed wire. A solid gate firmly locked. The chain: a chastity belt. Rusted padlock; security wax melted into the lock. A powerful guard dog with seven flaming mouths, so well-trained that it will savage something to death rather than bark. Don't wake the neighbor's cat!

A wasteland. At the bottom, three gates:

The narrowest one, the gate to paradise and written there: *Verboden toegang.*

Medium-sized, with a well-worn threshold, the entrance to purgatory. There is a sign here too: *No thoroughfare.*

In the middle, the widest gate, the one to hell. The sign here declares: Leave all hope behind, gossipmongers! this threshold is impassible.

Behind the metal barrier, a smiling woman — open-faced, expressing nothing but trust, courtesy, the most agreeable politeness — gestures to the passersby: Please take the trouble to come in!...

If you dared to look at it up close, this face would be nothing more than a mask; the body made of straw to the specifications of the most common taste and changing whenever it wishes; the naked hands, gloves the color of skin, on which (as evidence of prudence) the cuffs form extra mittens...

But where has the hostess taken refuge? — There, behind the spy hatch, holes for pupils, two black dots of mistrust (mathematical dots) are on sentry duty, perpetually on the defensive.

And right at the back of the gap that's there for breathing, despite the soul on patrol, the treacherous pink flash of a gnawed tongue flickers back and forth.

♥

Would you be afraid to show your teeth? to dare laugh without restraint, to react to the point of tears? What good would it serve? Your calm will also betray you: smiling belongs to women.

♥

But the green paradise...[54]

I was hoping that God would fashion a childlike world especially for the rest of us out of the leftovers of the universe, a varnished toy, shining, in colors without danger, image expurgated from life to be used by weaklings, innocents, soldiers discharged for spiritual deficiency, a world where the forces of nature and basic instincts, pain and rotten pleasure and all feelings would be simple pretexts, decorative designs imitating earth and water, fire and air, flesh and blood; where longitudes and latitudes would no longer atrociously bruise the globe... where the untrussed chicken, the criminal's wrist, the dog's neck will no longer bear blue-edged, reddened, peeled gashes... where the wasp, taking off its corset, will no longer rub its stripes, nor Saint X his stigmata... I was hoping... But God would not give way on this: in the way you know, here he even makes use, somehow or other, of animal, vegetable and mineral by-products, from his overproduction, from his factory of the absolute, from every unknowable thing.

What does a well-behaved child dream about, apart from the inhumane, the monstrous, the impossible? The ordinary. The most ordinary life has its adventures, its records, its wonders.

But with permission to skim, to skip pages, pages and pages — and to read between the lines, at leisure, as desired.

♥

Two well-behaved children

Let's try to hold on to our sorrow[55] until dawn...

See how it already transforms itself, molding itself into a mask of inexpressible grief.

On the brink of sleep, let us try to keep hold of it, keep it alive.

I want to deprive myself of joy and use it to nurture our sorrow. May it fatten itself on the least edible words in the dictionary. May it devour me. Hang over me. I want to feel it weighing down on my shoulders.

For I already trail too many corpses behind me.

Make it grow, little dream killer, make this justifiable reality grow. (This will be the least of your exploits.) You favor what is at the expense of what might be, that is your profession. So protect life, even if it is more amusing to kill dreams.

But it's over, you see, no need to think about it anymore. You have murdered all the sorcerers so miraculously that your superfluous blows are reddening your hand.

— Already an obedient child, still amenable. You will find him, dressed in garish colors, surrounded by happy toys; they are innocent, varnished, vulgar, possibly gilded...

You take him in your arms, and holding him up above the crowd, you show him the rich man's oldest son, his precious toys, antique, a gleaming patina, the sober sumptuousness of his clothing:

"Take a good look, little one, that is what you don't have. And everything else is bad taste."[56]

The well-behaved child put on his gray canvas smock and cleared the table of the books that covered it, of the agreeable junk of images. An unremarkable surface without anything questionable on it. Then, in front of a respectable wall, a good quality wall, he shut himself up in his dreams.

You took an interest in this. The amenable child talked about himself sweetly. Few thoughts resisted the scrutiny of your logic, the touchstone of an ideal of superhuman beauty. — When it comes to beauty, little lover of the absolute, are you not an infallible connoisseur?

Still obedient, the child despaired. But suddenly his despair inflames him. He clings onto what can never be made perfect, he will not let it go.

This naive intoxication made you smile: "You have fallen in love with a poison, a narcotic. Pain is so overrated, so out of date!..."

(Let's try to hold on to our sorrow until dawn...)

I didn't realize that the dream I foolishly placed under your protection was one of my last, little killer of love.

Little killer of loves, I had many lovers just a short time ago (all men were my lovers); you certainly knew how to separate me from them! Your divine skill shook each new pedestal, and the statue, no longer worthy of my devotion, crashed down at our feet.

What did it matter? Weren't you about to replace them all?

You stole away. You smashed the jealous God. (Oh! of course you didn't do it deliberately, and I forgive you.)

It's time you lost your power.

Out with it, show me how ridiculous my very obedience is. — What will become of me without her? (Does that mean without myself?) Nothing less, nothing more. Thinking to flatter you, I feigned a large part of my weakness.

I've always had, I always will have, a spare tyrant at the bottom of my heart.

Before I knew you were my guardian, I announced the downfall of your angelic rights.

Cancelled counsel.

Don Juan of philosophies, you sleep with little painted truths (you prefer virgins! Alas, mistakes and truths resemble each other all the more in that they are often deflowered, though rarely pubescent...) and you vibrate in search of your Reason's definitive spasm. But it is prudent and dry like a debauched heart that can no longer contract either love or faith.

Diseases remain. Watch out! Truth is woman: syphilis in the center.

Out of modesty.

If you look over my shoulder while I'm working, I will hide my schoolchild's notebook under the first novel to hand.

Give me some space. You hurt me. You can't understand that. Let's work it out. At a distance.

What does your absurd logic have in common with my supreme sensitivity? (I hate you! I'm confused — with all the changes of pronouns that our personal declension of silence and our conjugation of the verb "to love" imply.) What can be done, we don't resemble each other at all.

Yes, but...

We don't resemble each other at all: so much the better. One is enough in the house. *"One smoking in the house is plenty,"* said Bob.

♥

Me — to have Prince Charming, how childish! "To have" is not enough. Rather let us choose "to be."

Them — Is he really needed?

You — Admirably made for not getting on with each other!

Consciousness, the master carver.

My enthusiasms, my impulses, my little passions were irksome. You censure them, I give them up. Passions? Not even. Luxury activities most often not justified by the flesh. Only artifice in me, so little of the primitive. More greed than hunger. It's true, maybe you would have told me that hunger must be appeased, but greed requires correction.

Come on then! Divide to murder. Subjective dissociation. By a process of elimination, what is necessary about me? Certainly not the soul. Nor this desire, nor that regret. I promptly got over them. — The material is badly cut. I want it to be straightened up. A clumsy snip with the scissors. Bah! Let's even it up on the other side, we'll find an identical line (forget about cutting it straight!) A stain? We'll cover it up. Let's trim it again...

I no longer exist? Perfect! Now nothing can come between us.

The beast is dead!

No: the delicate mechanism of passions is completely broken, completely stopped, but little as she is, the beast has the harder life. A surge of instinct. This body should be pruned, branch by branch, member by member: call the surgeons.

(If they have to be persuaded, I can give them some precedents, those cakes that the Ferryman's Dog[57] likes best: Cybele's priests,[58] and your God himself, plagiarist of the pagans. "Your eyes offend you? Gouge them out. — Your hand? Slice it off... — The rest? It's very simple: castration!... Eh! what, now?... With your soul?... Shameless man! I've told you enough about it, make your own arrangements.")

After which, O concentration field of noble greed, our disagreement will continue with increasing strength as long as the odious carcass — which you have madly erected on yourself like a scarecrow — remains standing. Without wishing to, out of habit, I will act in the way that irritated you, in the same way. Without wishing to — with no excuse.

Obsolete body and soul.
You, the most generous of men, renounce false connections — or rather (because I definitely prefer to generalize): Society! It's all over between us.
Slaughter the beast!

Christmas Greeting

A style without inhibitions — a clear style. A style without authority — an insipid style.
Forgive, and give to me, so that I may please you with a forthcoming poem, give me, lend me, the esoteric qualities of the noun before the alarming frankness of the verb.

Young man with the peremptory thighs,
with the retractile soul,
(velvet cruelties)
and fierce inhibitions,
perpetual child!

Inflexible woman
with the rigorous caresses
(brutal laying on of hands,)
implicit, and assertive.

Never confess that you loved me,
— prove it rather
and gently disown all your tenderness.
I know too much,
(to believe your lying flesh)
I know the feline reserve of your heart too well.

I've been through all the hidden portals.

Whether impelled by the body or soul, would your secret actions
betray themselves, contradict themselves? No.
The spirit of compensation balances you.
It's: self-pity.

Sometimes, thanks to you, (fake death) I visit hell as a stranger.
Magnificent! A fog of blood-red smoke: storm or fire?... They were sucking the marrow from human bones (one of the damneds' little amuse-
ments — how tasty!) — Then... lurching waves, aggravated splashback
of flames, and their spume of sparks. Then... nothing more.

Your peremptory thighs,
your retractile soul
of feline reserve.

Be prudish and be brutal
(At ease, little friend!)

What would happen to us if we had to ask you
for permission to displease you,
Your confession, your disavowal
— when you yourself know very well
how to pay no heed.

Eternity
without you, without me, we have no use for it.
We have this moment which forces itself
upon us, without mercy,
which limits us and is incarnate in an omnipotent void,
this categoric imperative.[59]

Crisis of virtue.

(Don't let's exaggerate anything: as if I was going to take myself at my word!)

It's the river and not the pond.

It's harder to go beyond the boundaries of happiness than those of suffering. The attraction of the outing is always the same: you leave to explore what is to be found behind the wall, beyond the turn in the road, and turning, from torment to torment...

If this is only a progression toward some laughable happiness, what good is it! What good is it if the mind doesn't take part in it? And if it does enter the current, the futile current that produces nothing, if it bathes in the river — who will stop it from sinking there?

You took me in your lakes,[60] Ether...

It's another joy! — Static. Ataraxia.[61] The same suffering that once laid me out has become inconsequential. Will it rise again? I notice it without stopping at it. Hell has no more secrets for me, no more torments.

I see God in slow motion.

Later I will say what it is all about, what it is that the bearded Woman makes such a mystery of, I'll unmask her famous trickery.

Later.

I'm waiting 'til I get the upper hand.

Divide and Rule

(Desire pleasure): Love — Chastity: (alma[62] calm), O irreconcilable ones, would that someone other than me might decide between you. I want to grant you equal power in my country, establish you as sovereign twins of this kingdom: my life and its reactions. But constitutional princes — that's enough. Charming tyrants — or abdicate. What pleases me about each is what distinguishes him from his brother. In both I prefer excess, being the nearest thing to the absolute.

Equilibrium is our law.

> I have never known how to sew with
> a thimble, nor — tightrope dancer
> — make use of a balancing pole.

Circus of love. Modern comfort. You can walk without danger on this tightrope — dance without falling into the void. That horrifying void: indifference. The child draws his bow at us. Beneath our toes, the thread of our life, as supple as a serpent, but a pathway that is narrower than our feet, suffers and sags, vibrating with the urge either to snap or attack. Raw nerve against nerve, any superfluous

urges that thwart the main point — to keep upright — must be sub-
dued. Erection of the entire body. Vertigo... but the nets down below
are ready to receive the clumsy. Net of friendship, even, when the
need arises, net of hatred...

With you there is always a feeling one can fall back on. With
you, because you know all about substitutes for love.

Will I complain that I was trapped in exasperation's net so many
times? What body could endure a similar fall: from this high rope
(position superhuman — posture obscene) to the indifference of
reinforced concrete?

Exasperation saved my life.

You know how to retain us. With you, the string of the famous
bow, (with you?... I am assured that it is still thus!) the string is
composed of many smaller strings.

Monday, February 2: Purification.[63]

(Love? — artwork on a slate. Swedish gymnastics. Come on! it's
time to close these brackets.)

End-of-year accounts.

Received and due, white columns. But you, to calm me down:
"Our budget is balanced." No, now I can see red figures, lining up
accusingly — my debt.

What good is Christmas?

I go to you with empty hands (toys that move). But you: "What a child likes more than any other present is a live animal with un-predictable grimaces, surprise movements and which can be broken repeatedly." Maybe, if you wanted...

If I were to offer no resistance. Pointless resolution. You know very well that I will always escape you. My regrets quickly turn into malice. An intonation, an adjective, are enough to make me, versatile and monotonous, go from trust, from gentleness, from docility, to obstinacy, to "as for me," to an anonymous stare. Deaf, mute, blind, I wander around and, like a coward, leave you burdened by a dead weight.

How everyday my soul is! I find myself wearisome, and am only attached to myself by my errors, to my unpleasant life by its worst habits. A real adhesion. And you, just to say something: "Isn't every day a feast day?"

Tomorrow. Make tomorrow the most irreplaceable... Yes, I know that song. — However feast days, no less than the everyday, have sec-ular traditions. They differ only in their frequency. Fever, intermit-tent madness, madness none the less. If you flee in a circle, aren't you pursuing yourself? How can you escape perpetually returning, from the shabby return of even our own heroics?

On the 24th of December in a future year, on some unknown date, in a thousand years time beneath a different face, will I still, will I still have to go again and again to you, empty-handed?

I would like:
To be sufficiently similar to you, never to shock you, displease you, argue with you, ask for your forgiveness — or mercy.
To be sufficiently different from you (and from me), vary enough,

that you would recognize yourself in this man, from afar and from on high, ridicule without repercussions.

I would like to mean little to you yet make you smile like you-know-who, who doesn't know it.

I would like to amuse you neither more nor less than the unexpected negative, dictionaries, a fish out of water, the decadent morals of mechanical animals, the street where everything happens, where everything goes by, where nothing knows you.

I would like to merit being observed by you with as much curiosity, as much detachment, as the gods, as the dolls of the human soul.

I would like nothing to distinguish me from the things you are indifferent to...

For the rules of the social game (which I would like to change) are such that I never once win a hand against the rest of the world, and never win against you, against us — against the best of myself — without cheating.

I would like... I want.

But the other is already waking up: I am alive, alas! I am ill, I am demanding (of you, not myself any more), I am thirsty for everything that isn't within arm's reach. At the edges of the past, I wallow in pointless recrimination and it keeps me away from not only wanting, and choosing, but (in consequence) accepting your help. I push myself to the limit, I finally realize it, and for want of anyone better, complain about me to myself: I believe I've only got myself to blame.

But it's you who endure it, listen to it, see it when you have to (I show it to you).

Once more, you have read it, you are reading it, you will correct the mistakes I make in French.

When it comes down to it, everything ends up on your shoulders.

VI

X. Y. Z.

Never drop the shadow for the prey.[64]

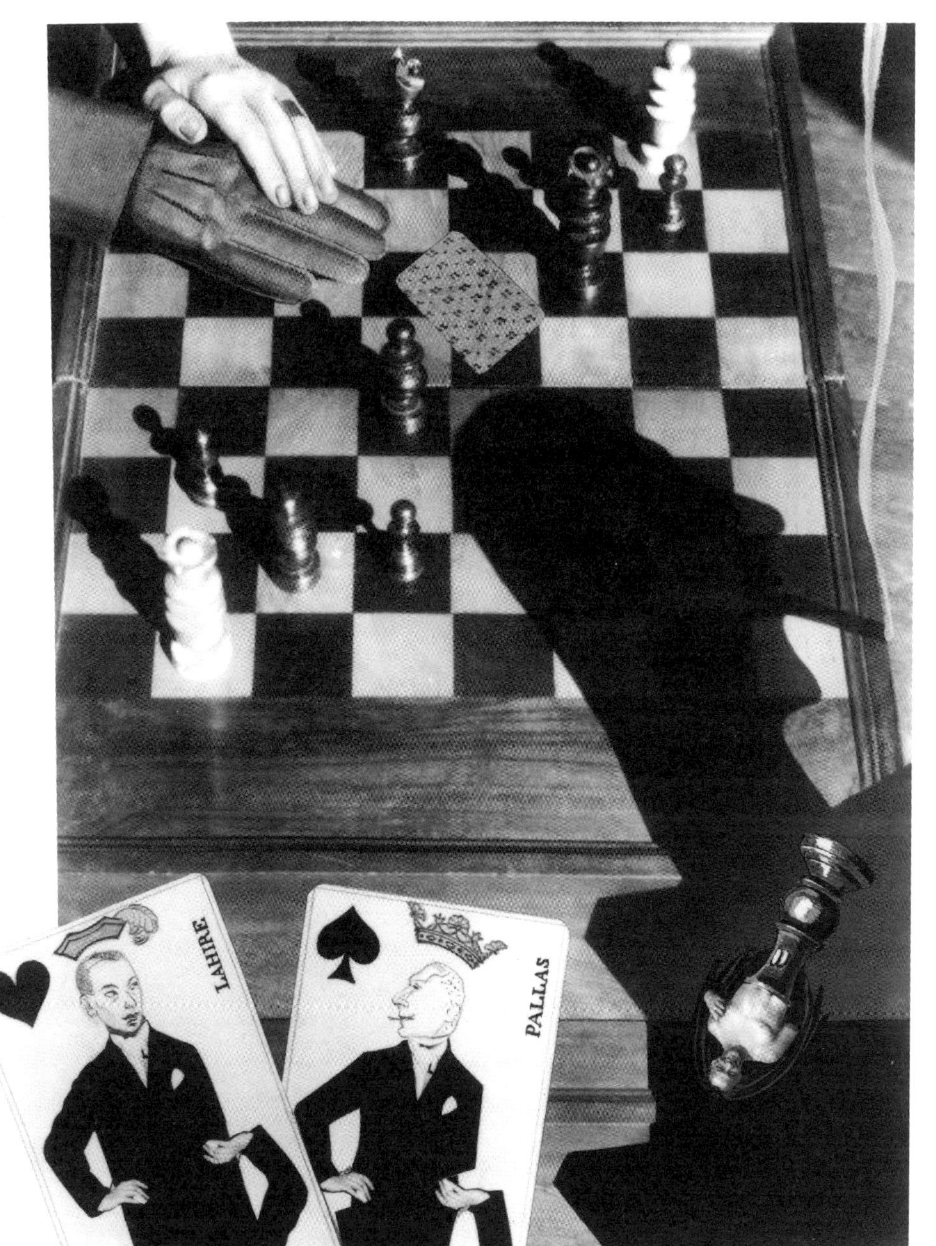

LAHIRE
PALLAS

SINGULAR PLURAL

Us.

"Nothing can separate us."

Declarations of love: sincere lies! (If you don't agree to play the fool every now and again, as often as I want you to, give up all thoughts of marrying stamens and thorns. The pink magic will be for others!...)

In the final reckoning we are forced to rely on the unknown, with a great algebraic X.

♥

Pink magic.

Absolute egoism is a refuge. I will often return to it. But with these games, I intend to lead lovers into treacherous harmonies, to the perilous pact of those who go about in pairs.

Love. The act itself is the creation of the flesh — flash of heat, a star so brief there's no time to formulate a wish, we're scarcely sure we even glimpsed it — but everything that engenders it, everything it implies, all the good old theater wires, are the creation of the mind.

The actor can make use of his partner, better: his enemy, as of himself; and it will be reciprocated.

But as soon as they have become one, in order to carry on the struggle and to be able to carry on provoking each other, they will have to cheat, dream up some accomplices for themselves. Beyond complete narcissism, the couple splits into two. We come out of our splendid isolation, lend ourselves to the world. My lover will no longer be the subject of my drama, he will be my collaborator. For the hero, for the heroine and for their conjunction, we will have to go down on the street and look for role models. Go separately. Masked. Make a new skin every night,[65] and a new landscape. This is the price of our duels.

Leave our defeats behind. Imitate, pretend to be the first one who comes along that pleases you and suits me, reconstitute the diamond of a look, the charm of these passersby. I am one, you are the other. Or the opposite. Our desires meet. It's hard enough just to disentangle them.

Are we there? Armed with things unknown, with false situations, with deceitful words and gestures, we will finally unsheathe our tongue from its kiss. Untie to tie once more the mortal embrace.

The art of infidelity: in you, whatever he might be, Prince Charming will be my easy prey. Everything depends on your artifice and the force of my desire.

♥

I am copying out this exercise (that my partner wrote in the required time and my own hand) to show how we seek to define our characters. It stands to reason that according to the mood of the moment, humanly indicated by our own physiology, the most abstract stance can and should be altered. Every living being — Russian doll, nest of tables — is supposed to contain all the others. The dominant and sensitive aspects of the character remain. It's only after a large number of exercises (whose value is completely relative like the following), it's only when we resign ourselves to necessary partialities, that we can allow our masks' molds to set. To clarify the still uncreated role we can draw on all sorts of pretexts: society games, absurd investigations...

Undoubtedly, in this case a more vulgar subject would have better served as an example. I opened another drawer... No. It was too much to ask of me.

♥

Let us roughly establish the reactions, even the least profound, of some amongst them to the announcement, exterior for some, interior for the majority, that God is in the anti-chamber, that he[66] is requesting they give the most honest account of themselves. We will see their attitudes in many other regards more clearly as a result.

Paul: I'm going. (Evading himself so as not to become emotional): This had to be seen. A unique opportunity. (Demeaning himself deliberately, for fear of being his own dupe): It's someone worth cultivating... etc...
Egon (in a blank voice): I've already told you that I won't be there for anybody.
Henri: Was it only because he wanted to have me that he put himself out? But it's me that will have him. Is this gentleman looking straight at me? Fine. I can take it.

<>

Genica: Let him come in. I'll receive him with pleasure. He is most obliging. My very best friend. But what the devil is his name?
Jacques: Let's admit him. And what then? Couldn't he have come straight in without making so much fuss?

Edouard: This is bad timing! What's he going to think of me: I was just dreaming about him...

Georges: He's too big! He's too near! He's too loud! I'd be of more use to him if he disturbed me less, if he backed off a little.

Eric: The clumsy oaf! He's flunked his entrance. Bring on the next act.

Reutler: They should put him in a straitjacket.

Charles: So be it. Man to man, we'll always understand each other. I'm ready. But we have nothing to say to each other.

Erich: Does he dare come to my house? I wouldn't mind telling him exactly what I think of him.

Oscar:[67] *His place is not in life but in art. Will you tell that person I am expecting him in my next book.*

Bruce: *Formless thing! Let me hold up a mirror and a song. Beauty is better than any gods.*

Jim: *Never felt that. It's queer!*

Alan: *I never!... (laughing)*

Georges: He's in my skin. It's an old acquaintance.
Jack (he trembles and weeps): *I have knocked him out many a time. I am afraid.*

↔

Arthur: If he presents himself under a false name again, you'll tell him I don't give a damn about him.
Paul (on his knees — and before what, Lord!): Here I am. I was waiting for Thee.

↔

André: Bolt the door. If anyone lets the unknown give us the slip, I'll bump him off.
Robert: He's bluffing, your Unknown, still an underling. If only he'd be polite at least; if he'd just decapitate himself before entering, and put the other sex, virgin too, between his legs. — A fine gesture, indeed, and one which would touch us.

↔

Swann: *Hand me my gloves, will you? Now let him in.*
Mitchell: *I am busy. He can wait.* (He's got all the time in the world to wait.)

↔

Robert: *He has so much to do, don't let him wait.*
Ruprecht (looking at his watch): It's fine. He's punctual.
Fernand: He's turned up at just the right moment. Of course. One always has to put oneself out for that animal. Anyway... he'll have to take me as I am.

↔

Donald: *He never wants to see me. It's just one of his tricks.*
Jack: *He cannot be with you all the time in the state you are in. He's never all there with us. But we must be thankful for small mercies.*

☜

the R.P.B.[68]...: No. He asks too much. Let him try next door. I already gave him something yesterday.
the pupil R.M...: Let's bet that he speaks to me in Hebrew. I'm going to get an interpreter.

☜

André: Is this the same man? I don't recognize him...
Jean: He's already in the place. He couldn't be any nearer.

☜

Bob: *I don't need him. He'd better mind his own business as I do mine.* (And when Bob starts speaking French: I don't know what to do about that kind of thing. I wish it would just get lost!)
Me: I don't eat this kind of God.[69] It's not him I'm waiting for, it's the Other. (God leaves. I felt him leaving...) — Hang on! Get him back. I wasn't ready to receive him, I am not worthy of him. If only he would come back: I love him.
You: It's for Claude. He will like it and I don't really want it.

☜

This exercise is worth my while as long as it's useful to us. But afterwards...

"God" is elastic. Define your terms. ("Holy Spirit" isn't appropriate either.) Each gives the name "God" to whatever seems good to him and will never admit what it is, what futility. (I am using this word quickly while my angel is elsewhere. He would have hidden it from me. If I had glimpsed it despite him, I wouldn't have been able to grab it. He'd have confiscated it from me.)

♥

EXERCISE ON TWO NOTES

Obscene curiosities.
P — I like this style of transparent card: the soul through the body.[70]
They'd be worth collecting.

Watertight bulkheads.
E — What I find most admirable about the Passion is not what you believe. I would sacrifice myself willingly for men, yes, for all men — but kiss this one, that one, like a brother? never! I'd get myself properly crucified for them, so long as none of them ever laid a finger on my skin.

E — In his place I wouldn't have had to look far for my Judas. You are never so thoroughly betrayed as by yourself.[71]

E — For those who value only mental, spiritual things, for a man attached to his contempt for the body, the tour de force is not to sleep with the leper but to greet the pharisee.

The relative kingdom.

E — My like? Neither conceived nor conceivable. A third must always be sacrificed for the monster analogy to be worth anything. We're only allies, only comrades through opposition — against others.

As soon as you isolate it, the species (in the concrete kingdom or the abstract kingdom), generalization, disintegrates; the Homeland breaks up into parishes; Paris into *arrondissements* (Russian doll); alone at last, the couple are flung apart,[72] I separate from you, the Aryan male himself renounces his solidarity with the Aryan female.

There are as many ways of being as there are stars; I wouldn't know what more to say... Even if there should be so many in each star (is it my fault if the absolute is beyond comprehension?), it will not make one more.

P — Meeting on a young girl's breast, on a cream tart. Concordance of choice doesn't imply concordance of tastes. Do we know what alien intentions brought our hands to touch each other from so far away? — Similitudes, sympathy? — Miracle? No: coincidence.

E — If paths cross, it's because they don't run alongside each other. Presumption of divergences.[73] Watch out for shifting railroad points!

Confession.

E — My childhood game. I preferred to be the horse rather than the coachman — especially when the friend who supervised our harnessing had a good whip, and knew how to use it.

Gott mit uns.

E — What idiocy! Ah! Rather: *Gott mit mir* — wonderful pride. However, since I've known you, "*Gott mit uns*" seems sublime to me. For one must not forget that "we" can mean a couple — that two-headed monster.

❧

The best way to keep your god near you: crucify him. The pagans who used to collect gods pinned Jesus to the cross like a rare butterfly.

❧

Idyll.
P — ... to be in a state of legitimate attack.[74]
E — ... following the shipwreck, cling to a floating mine.

❧

(P.) ... curious about a soul he experiences as alien and available, curious, and by definition, affable. "I am not so polite by nature that I can be nothing but polite. So I force myself — and overstep the mark."

❧

P — I am woman. Compassion puts me in the mood for consoling: making love. But since I am, after all, a man, and quick to attack, beware: this sort of thing doesn't happen without some brutality involved!

❧

Tomorrows.
E — Are you insulting me?
P — No, quite the opposite. I wouldn't have used that word yesterday. We weren't intimate enough. And I would never allow myself to use it with one of your compatriots. The value of the word "*boche*" is purely erotic.

Syncopation.[75]
From the same to the same (with tenderness):
God! How ugly you are!

Nothing but the flesh...

E — Do you doubt my modesty?
P — No: I know about switchblades.

E — If you see me hesitating at the edge of pleasure, come and help
me: remind me that I love you.
P — Love puts the least naive man in such a state of mind that he
asks his executioner for help.

E — Handsome? Me? — Yes: as if to say a handsome syphilis.

Out of respect for humanity.
E — Due to suppressing my passions, I've contracted a distention of
the heart. I demand urinals on all public highways.

Minima buys at the Minimum.
E — How to be happy?
P — (A little love?...) You can't fool me: imitation pearls!
E — Perfect imitation. Can you tell? Anyway, it's more sensible: admit that you want to sell them, give them away, that you'll let them
be taken or lose them... Say thank you. No? You are wrong. Do you
want to be loved at face value? Frenchman! Your heart's behind the
times. In our times, you need to know how to be happy on the cheap.

P — Find a common denominator in words, things and people (in love). With one throw of a stone hit as many things as possible.
E — If you try to hold too many things at once, your grip will fail.[76]

E — Learn how to place vampires to bleed people. But if they haven't had their fill they'll be hard to remove.

A proposal of marriage:
P — I will take the place of variously girthed snakes for you. My torso will replace the ones that fill your arms in an embrace. My thighs will obey you, well-cast reptiles; once more will you have those monstrous swallowers of mice; you shall have my neck, my ankles, my wrists; and my fingers, at your whim, will be grass snakes or common vipers.

Don't concern yourself with formalities: I'll take care of those. Heaven is missing its wings; and God no longer requires the consent of the motherland to facilitate the union of bodies and souls.

Anticipation.
P — It was enough just to trace a line in chalk: the little chicken followed, fascinated... frontiers of good and evil, of France and Navarre, levelled in the macabre dance, erased by the brutal stamping of the human race, I hope you will stop making such a strong impression on people. — I take the blame: we spend time talking of you.

   Last wish.

P — Her well had gained a bad reputation, but because she wanted us to continue visiting her, she covered the entrance to it with branches and leaves...

Be assured that I seek not Truth; but if by misadventure I fall into her trap, may she receive me naked, flesh well upholstered to absorb the shock.

Touch wood, the impotent's precaution.

P — Provided that it's properly tempered and penetrates your flesh deeply, I'd like to be on the blade's side.

E — German loyalty, German strength, German venom... only the sting of the national wasp is fatal (where you live bees have buttoned foils!).[77]

I deliver myself unto you disarmed — for fear of being defeated with my own weapons.

Intoxicated.

P — I need your sting, stupidity, my snake bite, discord and everyday malice. We become so used to it we can't do without it. Our equilibrium is an amalgam of poisons. — Sleep seeks to deceive us... (wait, my sentence isn't finished)... I'd sooner suck a bee's sting than give in.

Love cheat,[78] who's being deceived?

P — A hen takes our vulgar trickeries under her wing and agrees to blend in the same tenderness, or the same irony, bantams, ducks and shellfish — porcelain, heart of stone, dense wood, seedless gold, April fool, Easter sweets and the entire inventory of trompe-l'oeil...

Why won't this viper sit on my dove's eggs lovingly? If only to eat them cooked to perfection.

⌖

Bad *goalkeeper:* I'm only good in attack. It would be most unwise to entrust me with the defense of a body — above all my own.

The hereditary enemy: On the other hand, you would defend my country very well.

⌖

Politeness.

E — ... be just as generous in accepting what is given to you.

⌖

Variation on a well-known theme.

P — Place where snakes converge, I love to hear you advocating devolution — but watch out for your frontiers!

⌖

Metropolitan.

P — We obviously live on the imaginary line that goes from EUROPE to CONCORD.

⌖

Alarm bells.

P — ... your skin color of sand...

E — Color of quicksand where people get stuck... Come on, don't be frightened: I'm not saying it to tempt you.

P — Too soon: you fired with no plausible motive.

The happy man.

E — You don't have the right to insult me like this; you must earn it.

P — Give me some credit, I always win. The most cautious usurer lends me money on a lottery ticket.

Explanatory note.

P — ... General events act against me (distinctive ones work in my favor): war, volcanic eruptions, Spanish flu, military service, etc... But what am I talking about? I'm still alive. Even earthquakes wish me well — like opportune bumps of the vehicle sustaining my pleasure, maybe one day — who knows? — making it last forever...

The adversary — See Messina and die... What's keeping you from registering our luggage?

Greed.[79]

(P.) Nature was never enough for him, he always had to extend it in some way. He'd have to have: the hermaphrodite, the threesome, the four-leaf clover, the five-legged calf, the star with six points, the night of seven days, the eighth heaven — eight deadly sins — the nine-hour day, the cat o' ten tails, the decimal-plus-one system, the worker at the twelfth,[80] thirteen strikes at midnight — and make love at six.

The practical man.

P — Only make use of troubles, disgusting things, ruptures... I make my desires happen. Can you ever have too many?

E — You're showing off.

P — Only transmute our disappointments.

E — Alchemist, by what right do you sublimate[81] me?

P — By no right at all. I don't go in for that effect.

Don't fidget!

P — You'd like to move away from the fire — without looking as if you were. No: flee courageously! You won't escape me through the sentimental window, even if you stitch our sheets together. My flesh overflows onto my soul, onto my life. Everything that touches me is infused with it. Even my shadow is made of it, and the traces my feet leave on the ground, that my mouth leaves in the sky. The prey makes its mark. — Why let me go for a shadow as solid as myself?

Automatic revolver.

E — Did you see that one too? Have a good look, take in every detail, don't hold back on my account!...

P — I assure you that it's of no consequence.

E — I know. Nervous twitch. When you make love to them, it will be the same song.

The husband turns a blind eye.

E — I have a dentist's appointment (or: My country needs me — or: I've run out of cigarettes). I hope my absence won't inconvenience you too much? I can send someone to take my place.

Life in the garrison.

(E.) Between two religions, such boredom, such inactivity! Demobilized, arms dangling, the mystics drag their sheathed spurs over the public promenade, imperialism without a job, barracks-sick...

God offers them a lovely uniform, intrigue, great big horses, daily stultification...

Insulted, furious, the pure ones and the deserters receive their souls every morning on the end of a boot — cursing their own selves if no one else is around, swearing at the reveille instead of their own persons.

It's very important to keep the heart busy during the dead season.

But
I will lighten your load, volcano: I'll feed myself with your lava.

P — I've quashed your enemies, Serpent! I'll have to suck out your venom like the milk of a reservist mother, of a thoroughbred bitch. For if your breasts became heavy, sterilely inflated with the blood of war, with the sperm of hatred — in peace, in love, I would never see your pure form again...

From now on who could tempt us, reviving the paradises we abandoned, the abandonments we lost? Faded with the beauty of the serpent as far back as the memory of our youth...

Why return to the gardens of Eden at all, without the inventor of sin (man will never come up with it alone), without the thrill of the risk and no hope of recidivism?

Man will never come out of it alone...

Withered adult, child lamenting the belly of its mother, the poet still calling to his muse, the dreamer to his guardian angel, Saul to his seven handsome demons, the painter to his model, and without a compliant body, the lover wouldn't know how to invent new positions.

⟢

Here, Snake! (I whistle.)
P — If it's really the demon's fault that we're lost, he alone can save us. One is only ever cured of an illness by the same woman.

⟢

I tame the figure seven.
P — When Satan is the animal familiar, the tempter deluxe, — lap dog, pocket dog — no longer of Eve but of Man:
— Down, serpent! Down! Be chaste, chaste... Good. And now beg.

Break him in slowly.
Private sin, domestic demon, come: I no longer fear you.

⟢

Paris Ham

E — It's not about those who consider their navel the center of the world (a weakness that only oppresses oneself). It's about those who consider the world to be the center of their gravity and treat it accordingly — that is: with shameful indifference.

But can the sphere be left to its own rotations? Other than by the lash of the whip, how can the earth be made to spin?...

Would I dare judge (Take Care: Dangerous Bend) those who — maybe to fill their own purses — acquit me of crimes horrible to premeditate, for the execution of which an admirable enlargement of the heart and fists is humanly necessary?

Let he who knew how to sin utter the first insult. If pig there is, it's a show pig. So be it. May they take Europe for their navel, may they mix up the universe and their stomach. But let this stomach be a cared-for stomach, the muscular lyre of an athlete, the flesh and skin of a whore.

⬿

Omissions

E — There are people who would make you sick with their ugliness.

P — Don't challenge me: I'd end up strangling you. When it comes down to it, you have a very slender neck. It could be gripped in a flash...

♥

It's infuriating that one can only offer what one has, what one is.[82] But...

We cover our faces with masks, then cover them again, put on makeup, then make them up again, maybe only exaggerating the resemblance to, only accentuating the imperfections of, the hidden face... it's a waste of time.

Yet we wear ourselves out with these pointless games: it would be better to outbid everyone instead!

Elsewhere too makeup is a must.

WISHFUL THINKING

Before reading this page, make this wish with me: for words with double meanings.[83] A writer can only play heads or tails with words, as you do in secret with your most sacred feelings and principles.

Nineteenth century — have a heart.
Twentieth century — have the stomach.

Realism.
The mother was so unappetizing that the child was offered an aperitif before being served the breast.

Romanticism.
The flea — that vampire.

Surrealism.
The vampire, that flea...

Symbolisms.

(The day before yesterday): Get out of my sunlight.[84] (Yesterday): Get out of my consciousness.

Suspect.

... Would I have a sense of the ridiculous? Am I French without knowing it? Me — born of an unknown country.

Courage!

Attack my favorite values first, these are the most resilient. And the new order? Nature, abhorring a vacuum, provides for it fittingly, automatically and according to laws which are good to know about. Hit a head, a head appears. I'll say it again, it's about aiming high.

It's true, I should have thought first: you only throw something out to put something better in its place. Will this set a false precedent?

Another kind of courage.

The courage to be repulsive. Everyone should have been through it, in any case everyone will have to go through it. Our cowardice doesn't change anything about that.

Modesty.

Virgin and martyr? The highest degree of idiocy. Maybe being a martyr's not too bad... It could have its charm. But virgin!

Obsession.

— A virgin at ninety? No. But doubtlessly she masturbates normally, without any curious objects or taking hygienic precautions. For she is one of those women who, once married, close their eyes and do what they call their duty and get pregnant every time.

From all sides.

The traces left by man's activities are sometimes touchingly stupid, sometimes astonishingly wicked — depending on whether you're in the mood to cry with rage or tenderness. But no one should cry: everyone should laugh!

Laziness: The Sultan replaces his Great Eunuch with a Great Deflowerer.

He has taken the part (or his part) of virtue.

— The end is nigh.

Madrigal.

He performed an exemplary baptism.

What young girls dream of.

— Well, yes! You're always telling me off! I won't hold anything else against you since it's for my own pleasure (I mean it's for my own good!).

Mutual concessions.

One evening he beats his wife. The following evening she beats her husband.

Apteryx[85] victory.

The lizard's tail is fragile... But reviving the custom of the super-human (of his sixth sense), the Angel leaves his wings behind in the hands of Madame Putiphar.[86] On your mark... the bird flies off.

It's obvious! — Only the mind matters.

Go ahead, flay me: I won't feel any the worse for it.

A sentimental counselor.

The archer has no more arrows in his quiver. Nevertheless, he pulls back the string, he sets the trap. And each time his greyhounds have flushed out, run after, hunted down the beast, he turns toward us, turns to man for help.

But you cross your arms, sniggering:

"Rascal! Are you still hunting chickens — at your age! And are you still using such an unreliable implement in this didactic century? — Love, if you must prey on something, learn how to kill it outright with words."

Daphnis[87] or the weak-minded.

I have my desire at the tip of my tongue; but (I have such horrible memories) I'll never go back to the traditional act.

Devalue the race.

Men have tested the theory of inflation on their own flesh... Too many children on the exchange market. — The deluxe specimens are mine!

Soon to be released.

Having resolved to fall in love, I tried out diminutives of the eligible names, as a pregnant woman gets a first name ready at the same time as the unknown prisoner's layette. But it's double the work (you have to think of everything), boy or a girl?

Harlequin.

I was told so often I was heartless that I ended up accepting it.

A double-bottomed heart for illusionists.

If they measure themselves against someone they cheat — stretching themselves and standing on tiptoes.

The fox.

It was no use my kissing him on the mouth, he always moved his head away: "It's so that I can see you better, my child."

Let them have the last word. Avoid the resentment of discarded friends. I know some who willingly set themselves up on the same landing. You'll often get their news.

The passion of the plausible.

So that people will believe me, I don't say what is true — but what is plausible.

Reserves.

Beauty, beauty, the promise of happiness... Come on! You are far too discreet, too well brought up, too prudent, to make more than an allusion to the happiness a person might expect from you.

— Beauty, promise of torment!

Indefinite Perfect.

There are some people for whom the only ideal is to have a life that can be put in any hands.

From Normandy.

How would I feed a passion other than that for Good and Evil when my own soil creates webbed roots for the apple trees. My snake would not know which Eve to devote himself to among so many sour apples.

The mystery of this man: PUBLIC DANGER.

Do not allow CHILDREN to play with the LOCK.

The slip of the tongue.
Through some illusion of my erring flesh...

Piano lesson.
— I am completely inexperienced where love is concerned: I'm terrified of being clumsy...
— I prefer it like that. I've known some that started so badly!
— ...
— Ah? Too bad! Even on your own you can get into some bad habits.

Man of the desert.
Youth is his target against nature. He would get himself sucked by the sun to migrate to a world still molten.

Indirect method (to lead a young Protestant to confession).[88]
"Intermediaries are indispensable." — Even for the things of this world. You don't speak the language of God well enough to dispense with an interpreter. There would be some misunderstandings between you and your Creator. — And above all don't trust God, my child: (consult your Holy Bible). He has never honored the professional secret.

Sin with forethought.
— Do you shriek when you masturbate?
— No, Father, I pray...

One of Narcissus' heresies.

— Thanks!... and this isn't the first happiness I owe you.

We are only ever shown the hero's point of view. But what if I take a minor player's side?

Magic-City.

They make such a distinction between "active" and "passive" — imbeciles! May there soon be a "feminism" for cinedi.[89]

Origin of the blue chins.

Soiled glacier, sheets, the purity of the earth defiled... Turbulent hours. Our hair became so entangled that night, that in the morning — to end it — we had to have our heads shaved.

Sappho.[90]

— I'm going to buy myself some socks. — Do you really wear socks? — No... (what are they called?)... stockings. It's just a way of speaking really.

... Instinctively I looked for the buttons of my "fly" on the right (men's side), but the tailor (you have to tell them everything!) had sewed them on the left for me.

Mea culpa.

Write for a minority, the poet's fruitless work, stupid, vain yet somehow noble. But, oversensitive victim, you mustn't let yourself get walled in by the family, forced to write against a minority.

Purity is composed of all the stains, as white is of all the colors. But if just one is missing, motivation falters, harmony breaks down, the mayonnaise turns. Never hold back on green to the detriment of red, the sky to the detriment of blood, lust and pride in unequal doses.

Athlete full of vice. Specializing his soul, stretching himself out on a ray of the spectrum, is what they call "turning out badly" in angel slang.

A proposition for Lent: everyone who wears a mask the rest of the year should come out barefaced, unrecognizable.

Open up — and someone will knock.[91]

For those who have not been satisfied with their role on earth, God establishes a review panel:

I provide the theater, you choose your stage sets, your adventures, your character, your sex, your makeup... But the false accents you'll have used on stage will be reproduced eternally; and if you've kept your personality at bay, he'll let you have it back. Never having known how to let yourself be moved by your soul, you will never know how to touch it either. Strangers to yourselves, ridiculously followed or preceded by a marionette four regulation steps away...

Who gives nothing has nothing.

I am the first to acknowledge my mistakes: If you embody your ideal, I'll back you up. But what good is that to you? Didn't you have it already?

An indeterminate genre.[92]

There are people who morally speaking live from day to day. They follow the market price in newspapers. If the price of mocha dips, they love coffee, they force themselves to drink it. They show their paw, sometimes covered in flour,[93] sometimes in coal, reveal their business sense, their sense of what is artistic, based on what they take to be the flavor of the day. They seek angora angels, alley angels — if "angel" is profitable.[94]

But faced with unlabeled products, they become completely disorientated... A sticker is obligatory.

This verbal debauchery... These are their tricolored masses.

Other temperament, other moral values.[95]

"Open your mouth and shut your eyes!"[96] This is how adults became accustomed to perverting the young. Whose fault is it then if, after that, their women are weak, gossipy, and lacking in perception?

With me and most children, the expression of desire is mouth shut and eyes wide open. This shouldn't be abused. Mute. Unisensual. A variety of infirmities. The example is not well chosen!

Looking through the hole of the navel:

It isn't only his own that the child makes the center of the world. It doesn't matter what kernel keeps his flesh together. Mystery is the lock at which an eye, for want of anything better, serves as a master key.

Thus:

— Mommy! Why are the boats in the water, Mommy?

But the mother is elsewhere, out of the water, out of the boats, out of herself. The decentralization of her mind is complete. A tough social life has forced her to replace the "whys" with as many peremptory "becauses" as "so thats." She says (perhaps surprised by the color of the sky...):

— Because it's lovely weather.

Not arguing or giving up (for he realizes that he has received no reply), the child repeats:

— Why are the boats in the water?

"Only strike him, Doctor.[97] I will make sure to parry."

We must deliver ourselves bound hand and foot. There's no better way. Have we got the time, or the means, to check? We are forced to by the action and interminable interrogation of actors.

So many contradictory statements, lies, denials — and above all, surprising silences. But what good does it do to defend yourself? Attack is much more expedient. In his duel with Valentine the role assigned to Mephistopheles is an outdated role. Only Faust will have to face God's judgement.

Nothing more baffling than proof. Figures are a lure. Everyone knows some kind of trick. They get pulled out, pushed around, rounded off. It's so easily arranged: One player works with Moscow time, the other with the time in New York — and the round is played.

Numbers tell us nothing for they have no personality. Nothing in this world is as peremptory as the shape of a talking mouth confirmed by an expression... Insults will teach us more than the most sincere statistics which can be corrupted by a simple printing error.

Women, France, your happiness depends on the value of your senses, your psychology. The most petty details (however humiliating!) will reveal more about a being than his brilliant feats because they are more usually overlooked. — He sharpens a pencil; he wipes his nose; he sleeps; he has a fever... (he's giving himself away). After a thorough etcetera, if the man has proved charming, open your legs and shut your eyes. It's a marriage of convenience.

Other ways of saying it:

Man will have eternal youth sooner than immortality. He'll protect himself from decrepitude faster than from a pinprick. The "accident" too will take on a singular value, and whatever one does (unless one has become ferociously "protectionist"), the accident will inexplicably increase.

Solidarity.

Our life today is subject to so much administration, depends on such a large number of transactions and such a crowd of beings, that we will be insanely lucky if we don't find a murderer.

In any human enterprise the few, rare happy beings are given pride of place, illuminated, their qualities greatly exaggerated. These are the big jackpots to make us get some lottery tickets.

Divided up.

In our times, when everything is based on the installment plan, even happiness, where politics, money, love, are articles of faith, so much credulity is squandered in the course of the week that there's nothing left for bank holidays.

Gender confusion.

Politics and the erotic are reduced to the vocabulary of libertinage. Here are our relaxed jacks-of-all-trades: happy to discredit at one and the same time the good actions of bosses, their efforts toward conciliation, and the kiss on the mouth. Break it up, gentlemen, break it up!

Revolving table[98] (dream)

Seated around the green baize, diplomats, serious as children, sucking their pens, suckling their style, are drawing up the Treaty of Versailles in automatic writing. (Their noble sincerity will be highly praised.) A gust of ghosts: pigeon flies,[99] prison flies, nations fly...[100] So wise are they that they would hear me talking!

Among them however are some with ugly habits who let themselves go in the dangerous onanism of literary corrections.

Others have such rapid imaginations that the sylph leaves them, gasping, at the first revolution; their hand quite exhausted... Having thrown off their clothes, their weapons, then their limbs, one by one, they arrive naked — what do I mean, naked? very slender, having no form and no soul at the post of glory, torment or happiness.

But I have seen — could one believe that vanity of honor would be capable of usurping the place of basic instincts in this respect — I have seen the great German leader, short on dreams, copying from his French neighbor. A bit of luck for the Prussian that he himself was copying from his German[101] neighbor! Bent over their right fingernail,[102] beyond Good and Evil, soon they all looked like conspirators to me — and the table revolved in the direction of the hands of time, or rather space... But Who were they all copying? Whence the initial impulse? I am lost in this.

At length their outstretched arms impel their papers, folded like accordions,[103] toward the center where the invisible arbitrator gathers them up. Invisible to me, god incarnate for some, a judge with his head dressed red as shame, a scarecrow made of straw, man or destiny masked, providence's eyelids sealed with hymen membrane, a virgin to be violated, etc., for others. Gathers them up and shuffles them in his old bowler hat. And now, just like in innocent games, the lots are drawn to see who, who, who will be eaten.[104]

All paths would throw their thorny lasso over me, would crush me between their walls, would pinch me to death there, in their hinges. If their smiling jaws meet on the horizon... simple effect of perspective.

(Illusion and truth are twin children who have swapped their pink and blue ribbons so often that, by naming them according to their color, I would get them teased, even if I happened to be right.)

Close your arms, paths! on others or on the void. You will have wasted your time stretching out. I won't let myself be snapped in traps. I will stay at the crossroads, my arms like the cross. My body as signpost. Feet firmly planted against the temptation to desert my post, to follow the first passerby. Conscious of distances, boundaries, churches...

Perhaps, as a reward for my patience, a lost angel will ask me the way?

Stormy nights, if you want to stay on the bridge of a ship (a bucking horse trying to unsaddle us), you have to secure yourself firmly to some frontier post.

VII

H. U. M.

Before renouncing this world I will
dance before Herod, because he is
interested in my sleep and knew to
how compel me to retrace my steps,
to rethread my dreams.

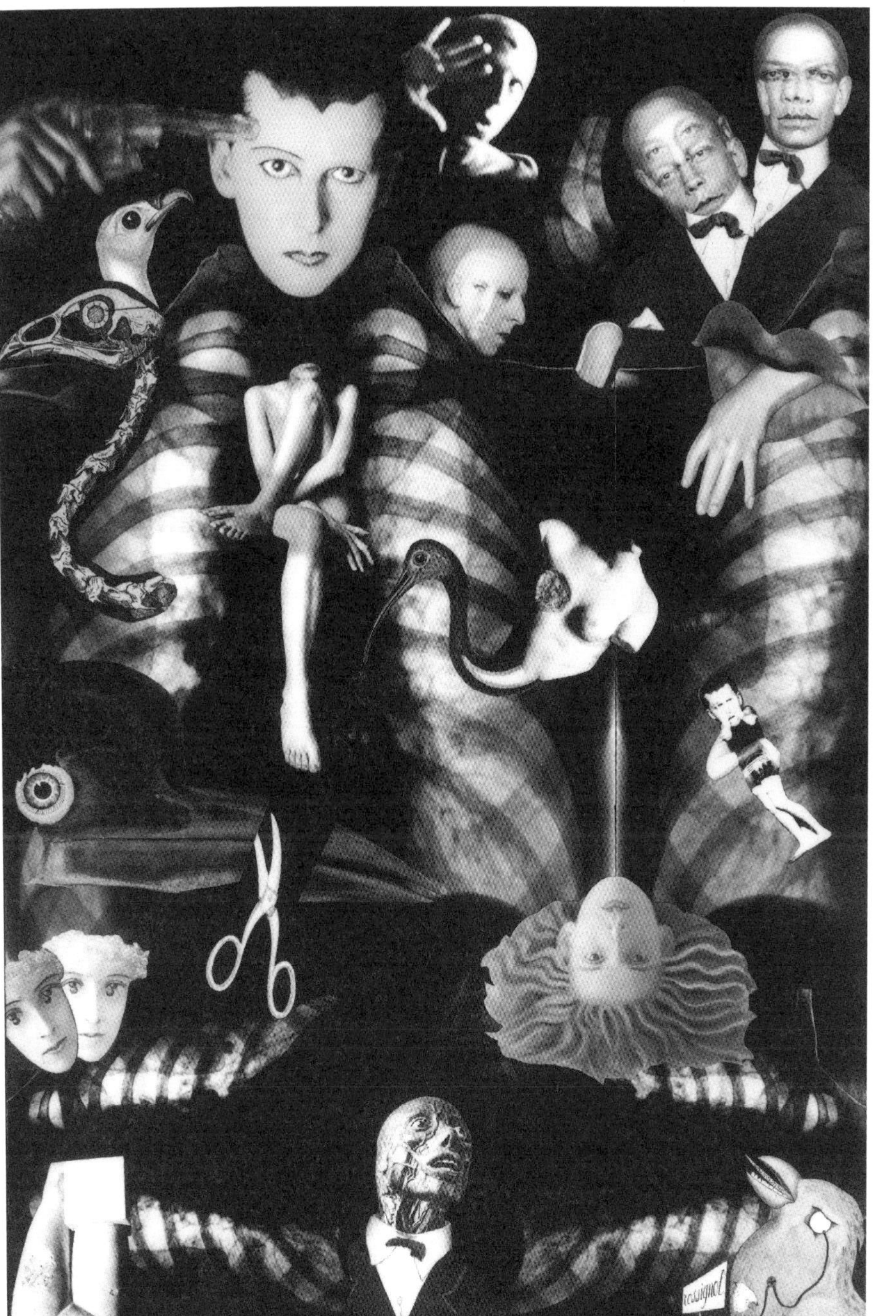

WRECKS

(Nightmare)

Curiosity keeps me awake in front of a man's face: skin pock-marked, battered, granulated — but white, but livid; the skull flat, the forehead covered in hemp; nose, mouth tumescent... The eyes vacant — the rim of a well, the well itself, colorless and with no intensity — the perfect horizon where I advance, where I am engulfed while an X-ray passes over my head... I do my best to believe that the image is out of focus; I contract, I dilate, I fiddle around with the astonished diaphragm of my eyes...

There is a silence between us, an obstinacy. It must be my father. He tries his best to understand and I to convince us — he, my own heart and this man... But I have no sooner felt that my destiny yielded, cracked, that infinity was restored to me, that I had seen a stop notch in the adverse abyss — in short: the click of longing — than I turn and flee, shouting, spitting out my soul, denying and renouncing my conquest, hurling abuse at my star.

I find myself walking in step, in step with my forgiven shadow. My breath, still uneven with some faded terror, offers me a transition... Can one give in to such monsters? and above all when in such a short time so many curlews' beaks have to be cut off!

After every café, all the even numbers, a stuffer of birds. More
easily than I had thought, and without leaving any traces, I pass my
fist, arm, through the window, and with my curved scissors, cut the
beaks off at their roots. It's hard horn, but not much more than my
nails... (Pussy makes no more fuss than me when she lets her claws
be trimmed, you know)...

Sparrows, seagulls, hares, partridges... None of them must be
left! — But the one I'm looking for, without knowing how it is made,
and just to see how it's made, is the nightingale's beak, with its false
teeth, with its painted tongue.

Concentration station, a regulating station. Arrivals or depar-
tures?... Is it my own departure making my mouth and eyes water?
Lies! — Fear, that's it, the mouth dry.

On a narrow footboard, scarcely a bread board, a safety board,
far from the luminous roof, far from the helpful platform, at the
switch rails of lines, between discs, signals, here I am, swept away,
lost. It's not a peninsula; I thought it was at first. It's a band of sand
surrounded by whistles, thunder and night.

I have overtaken my father and seek to convince him, through
whatever idea I can think of in the tumult, of my genius, of my
bravura... But I don't have time. His train comes in and doesn't slow
down. ("Your mother will be worried.") He runs, trying to drag
me by the hand, or rather I am trying to hold him back — dazzling
lights. The running board shines at high speed. I close my eyes...

Something falls which I still hold onto by a bit of warm, viscous
flesh, but my arm hangs limp.[105] Despair — and stronger, horror —
freeze me, and yet despite myself, I see, half relieved: It's a jointed
wooden artist's mannequin that clings to my fingers.

The drama was real without a doubt, but Chirico rescued me...
And I yell out this lie as gloriously and loudly as I can, hoping by
sheer insistence to force it on everyone, make it come alive (and my
father into the bargain): "It's a miracle! It was only a policeman!..."

To the glory of Freud.

So many people make love without knowing it — and love as mediocre, as botched as the prose of Monsieur Jourdain![106] — It's time to teach them how to do their job.

The ivory tomb[107]

A man had a confidant. He had to tell him about all his actions, all his thoughts. Any detail not told would have made him suffer remorse (sin of involuntary omission). Now, on his death bed this man had a dream — a marvelous dream that seemed to him to be the revelation of the entire mystery of life. He was in haste to impart it to his friend. The most beautiful legacy. But he could not regain consciousness. He struggled at the edge of a dangerous beach, like a swimmer swept away by the current... He regained his footing briefly — a ground swell carried him off.

He died without ever having woken. But the superhuman efforts he'd made and the horror of being forced to keep his secret had disturbed his soul. He died insane.

What do they do with madmen on the other side of the night? This is not foretold in Jehovah's statute books.

St. Peter saw a man arrive who was ceaselessly repeating the same unknown sounds (St. Peter doesn't know any French). He led him to God. God understood that the man had lost his reason and that he understood the Secret (for out of professional necessity God knows all terrestrial languages) — a secret that was considered rather blasphemous. God didn't get angry (he's heard plenty of others!) but he classed it: "obscene," and didn't dare put the delinquent in hell. For demons are shrewd and still corruptible.

It must be said that usually drunks are mixed up with madmen and are sent to sober up in the Inferno.

As it should be, God had an inspiration. The angels — who are patriots and from one little village and not like the demons who come from many different lands — only speak and understand Celestial.

God introduced the man to them and left him among them: In truth, he said, this is a new prophet magnificently singing Our praises. A false interpreter was assigned to the madman and charged with translating, and forced to imagine the recantation.

But on the festive day when God rewards his best flatterers, the man under attack regained consciousness and flew to hide himself in his unknown tomb, swearing that it was better to hold his tongue for all eternity than gossip like women — and serve as a loudspeaker for divine, or even human, imbecility.

Selling one's soul to God: is to betray the Other.

Late-season fruits.

The blood orange has its admirers, who suck it smugly. Cooks stalk it; they'd like to put it in some tartar sauce. However, some, like me, turn their noses up. In silence they mold bits of bread into balls, delighting in their work, then chuck them in God's face.

The call[108]

Heaven's threshold is black; white, the panels of the narrow door. Here and there bleached sepulchres, loosened stones the color of quicklime. The angels got into the house of the dead by breaking and entering, forcing their way into funerary monuments, tombs, coffins, urns... But the serpent race watches over us and encourages the flight of souls and bones...

The clarion calls. Standards rinsed with laundry blue line the path of duty. Arms are presented to God. A military register is taken. Woe betide the poet who might reply "absent" when his name is called, the unnatural soul that might fail to recognize his body.

The stateless men desert in great numbers. Their last game of hide-and-seek. Gabriel is down below; searching in corners... Don't tire yourself out, my child. We can still be in absentia.

Once the police have gone by, each for himself rolls in the grass. Darkness spreads. Toads sing. The long and newly dead (in other words: the dead and the living) fraternize.

Suddenly St. Thomas, who has sharp hearing, gets worried: Who is being deceived? — and orders a patrol.

In haste, under threat, the damned come up with some tricks. They bring some rescue coffins. They stuff them in: Women and children first! And when they're too full and overflowing, the men of good will push down the lids by sitting on them with all their weight. The diplomatic trunk is shoved back into the shadows, into a burial vault, into a ditch...

No paradise, no hell. It's a matter of crossing the frontiers of good and evil without a hitch.

— The others? It's well-disciplined flesh. These are the same people who, from father to son, at twenty, say they are happy and proud to wipe the ass of a cannon.

E — Being pro-military — but like a children's maid.

Gravestone

(Extract from a dream)

Leaving the dog show, I visited the cemetery of the aesthetes:
vaulted arches of jade, agate, lapis... Here it is. I stand with my back
to it to measure it. My hand on my head, I feel for the edge of the
stone: 1m 59. It's made of frosted black marble, inlaid with white.
Two beautiful feet with long toes, the ring finger and the middle finger separated according to the ritual design of Jewish hands. Below,
this inscription:

HERE LIE
NAKED
THE LEGS OF A DANCER
WHICH DANCED
WHEN DEAD

Pigeon flies...
Despite their frontier posts, their home ports and good feelings,
the lands and the seas lift anchor.

Obscurantism.
God said: Let there be light! And there was light.
But no one remembered to add that it could never have appeared

without the intervention of shadow. He alone signed, but the Other was indispensable. We are familiar with this type of collaboration.[109]

NO MAN'S LAND

Day and Night.

Favorite disciple, the Lord's own darling, Satan revolted against his king. Was this the weary ambition of a spoilt prince, of a fictional pretender to the eternity of the kingdom, hereditary in vain? No, let us rather believe (we who may have been marked out already for a similar fate) that he suffered from perfectionism, from impatience with the limits of divinity, from a taste for the impossible...

The fact remains that he went off to sulk in the other celestial hemisphere, established his own kingdom there, anointed himself, acknowledged himself as its tyrant — fatally similar — and nevertheless (to what ends? it was neither better nor worse) refused to relinquish it. Daytime up there needed his night; but his light was exactly the same as the angelic shades.

The Assumption of the Demon.

People will revolt against any regime, no matter if it is the result of a revolution, even anarchy. One of Satan's subjects soon dreamed up another set of commandments and plotted against the prince. He was driven out toward heaven.

Vice Versa.

The desertions increased. From one kingdom to the other emigrated the malcontents. Each, depending on the moment's caprice, had himself naturalized either as an Infernal or a Celestial but peace got nothing out of it. (All the Germans can move to France and all the French to Germany but Berlin and Paris will be no less at loggerheads; Lorraine and the Ruhr will not confront each other less.)

There was a great reshuffling of Spirits.

The snow and its continuous softness of ever more abundant, less and less hesitant feathers, would meet without knowing it drops of damp shadow breathed out by Jehovah.

And that's all.

Confusion.

Unexpected embrace, an angel, a demon collided in the middle of intermediate space. A relentless struggle to start with, and yet they had no idea why. Quite simply their collision was inevitable. But this hostile embracing so strongly resembled love that they awoke from it brothers. Obvious conclusion: their rebellion is identical, yes, of the same nature. Spinning, waltz, vertigo, they lost their sense of direction. What is up and what is down? (Isn't the ceiling the firmest ground for a fly?). Gyration becomes their only thought. Attached one to the other they become part of the astral revolutions, merge, become rounder, fallen angel and fallen demon, allow themselves to be carried away, a sphere, red where their cheeks meet flushed with desire and shame for this erotic adventure...

But unsettling the order of the solar system, licentious comet, meteor, they fell quite by chance into the earthly paradise at exactly the same moment as the apple from Newton's tree.

The Tree of Good and Evil.

God deeply mistrusts heavenly gifts. None is better armed with suspicion against such presents than he. He picks up the meteorite, examines it... and hangs it on the next apple tree with a notice: FOR EXTERNAL USE.

Adam and Eve, agreeable marionettes, who only ever read with their eyes but are guided by an extraordinary intuition, felt (as indeed they should) the evening dew of desire rising within them.

Adam, simple child, stuffed everything that fell into his hands straight into his mouth. Little Eve, precocious girl, buried all her treasures in her private parts. In short, each devoured Good and Evil in their own manner.

Eve's body is contaminated (the only doubts she will ever have concern the best way to make use of it). Thanks to opotherapy,[110] Adam buys himself a soul at great expense.

Frontier Land.

The instinct for double revolt is part of Man. He drags his companion (fully persuaded that he cannot detach himself from her) to the equator — serpent flexible and stiff, indeterminate line, ideal sign — that so precariously separates the warring kingdoms.

He settles down there, surviving after a fashion and crushing himself, generation after generation between two armies, between flesh and skin, between the bark and the tree of Knowledge.

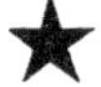

May it not be thus

The bread of our prayers is stale bread. The sky, a can of preserves. Not to mention the eternal soul...

That's enough about the present, I won't hock the future. There's no space to glorify our daily sins.

If I were God, that is god having repented, I would count my cadavers, my crossings-out. I'd make use of the harshness of done deeds to give myself a shock, to compel myself to bounce back to the devil... a trampoline is not a pedestal.

I would acknowledge the fact: What has been made has been badly made. That's the way with impurity.

I'd admit it: That's how it is.

But I'd decide: That it should be otherwise!

SALOME VANQUISHED

Haunted house.

A look? — Longed for. No, only eyes, cold eyes, multiplying because they cause me to suffer. They are vast: I will never cross this desert. Mirror,[111] that seems more cruel to me the more I burn and which refuses me the comfort of my reflection. Red which never overflows this mouth whose muscles never weaken. But won't each of its infinitely varied movements be always a new, always a similar rejection? (What were you talking about?... I was listening really well. — The ocean? Me too. — The ocean is you, you who engulf me).

I am hardly ambitious. Your mouth is too high up for me. But (out of stubbornness)... I will kiss your hand, Iokanaan![112]

The whiteness of hands, of all skin visible or guessed at. The phantom is complete. I possess a number of similar ones. Take your pick, my guests!

Do I create them myself? Certainly. This is how they are, this is how they will be indestructible. — Change dwelling? Can I do that? No more than a cat. — Change skin? The serpent's privilege. Eve only ever knew how to peel Good and Evil when they were presented in the guise of a universal apple, not in her own heart.

I won't leave it: I can't see how one can leave one's own self. This house, this obsession, there's only one remedy — set light to it.

Willful arson. Society, you will acquit my memory. I didn't act out of self-interest (you will say: lack of discernment). I didn't have any life insurance.

MORE FEAR THAN GOOD[113]

Demolition enterprise:
Is that really to my taste, my love? It's a stopgap. I would like to build something. There would be no shortage of materials. It's my plan that is unsatisfactory. — When you are looking for shelter, why make things complicated? To justify my house, which would take up little space, would it suffice that I consent to live in it myself?

Bad habit:
If I cannot consent to it, it's proof that I no longer know how to live alone. What a state of affairs!

For want of anything better:
Does the world have to be badly made for a being who is odd, but sexually sociable, to be forced to take refuge in crime as if it were a convent, not only to live in it, but even to create some new values there!
But what kind of crime?... What does it matter! A dead end.

The confession of my shame:
Will I blame the circumstances, my contemporaries? These aren't the circumstances of my life, these are its causes that led it astray. I was condemned before I was born. Executed in absentia.

The unnatural ones,[114] the real ones:
No more impossible metaphysics — let them be consigned to the accessory shop: theatrical costumes. But impossible physiques remain with us, alas! — or thank God! — really tragic ones, with no theatrical strings.

Shyness?

Being in love, I remain stupid about it. I don't pursue, but no more do I flee — for fear that he will imagine I wish to be pursued... This isn't modesty, it's cowardice. It's best to confess it. I wouldn't know how to impress anyone.

You won't be able to escape it: neglect is still action; it's the opposite of it, Pilate.[115] Negative flirtation has all the inconveniences of the other sort without any of its pleasures.

Massacre game.[116]

Fairy tales are no longer in season. All my stories, all my heroines end up in moral turpitude, in downfalls. But it's only proof by *reductio ad absurdum.*[117]

What do you want! You can't have this ending anymore: "They lived happily ever after and had lots of children." There are already far too many in the world.

Repopulation:

There are some people — probably the same ones — who would still yell at us: On to the very end! like during the war... Is it for me, their victim and their prey, to howl with the wolves?

Always her:

Set a good example. It's not easy. In order to encourage oneself in this, treat what doesn't yet exist like an obsession, think about it every day. Will I achieve the longed-for result?

I am sulking...

A child, like in the past: You refuse me soup, I will deprive myself of dessert. — To punish you and test myself.

But who am I hoping to punish now? Is it God?... And what use is this vain discipline when it's used against my own self? It's the right time, through death, to train oneself to live!

False departure?

Paris, April 25, 1925.

To the Chief of Police
of the   arrondissement

Dear Sir,

This is to certify that, taking advantage of the absence of my governess (who this Sunday has gone out to worship at the Church of   , accompanied by my seconds,[118] Mr.   and Mr.   , at   Street, no.   ), I have administered death to myself, alone and without any help — WITH PREMEDITATION.

The reason for this act, or if you prefer its pretext: the chronic sufferings of defective health. (I'm such a good liar!) My mind has certainly undergone the contagion of my body — or vice versa. I make no claim to anyone's respect, either in general or particular. I only ask that you conduct yourselves in such a way that neither my family nor my friends are made anxious — I am necessarily about to disturb them rather... (Necessarily? and the pauper's grave?)

I thank you very much in anticipation and ask you to believe in whatever available gratitude I've got left.[119]

Let me be!

Yes, false. How to prevent a wreck going by, oneself from clinging to it. Keep from us, oh, Lord, our daily bread — that we at last might fast in peace!

— Crime or suicide? Ask Nero: Theater! As far as I am concerned this could easily be a matter of emotional blackmail: You rejected me, etc.

Stance against nature:

Dressed in a sack (propriety must be observed) and lead weights on his feet, he threw himself into the Dead Sea.

He will float, thanks to the salt — to the salt substitutes, to the sunken cinders of tarry towns...[120]

It's over. I live on feebly, clinging to words, to fables. Clinging to the dead, to great names, to those disasters in which I claimed to see my vanity, my ruin and my damned remains, justified by the Conqueror's rage. (Among so many confessions, what a ludicrous confession. I'm wrong to emphasize it. It would be best to let it all pass unnoticed.)

However, I don't feel right. Without doubt: my soul has become ingrown[121] like a nail nobody has bothered to file regularly.

In all of this, who is to blame? Just for once, let's be French:

Bad government.
Certainly! In democratic heaven, God would soon be outvoted.

An idea which undresses itself. I guarantee it. It was delivered to me naked. I am only responsible for the swimming costume (designed by So-and-So).

It's not enough to be vanquished, you must also know how to turn defeat to your advantage.

Finished, mortal, relative.

Joy and pain. At last here they are, the parallels that meet in love. But love is not the infinite — quite the opposite, it's the thing most certain to be finite. In the realm of the absolute, there is no such thing as chance, such encounters would never take place.

All will be explained later...

Maybe they wanted a marriage of convenience? But for many years, the family intervening, no agreement could be reached: working out the dowry, warranty, division of possessions...

The advantage of rape is that it dispenses with the need for a contract. Same with wars, same with revolutions, I cannot reject attenuating circumstances. To unite or affect a reconciliation, modesties can only consent to the necessary concessions, sins of pride, humiliations — in silence.

It is so much more simple to act than to speak. Have I ever heard the opposite? For myself I'm interested in making the game more complicated. Those who live by their tongue have discovered a way of talking that replaces action, that's even more simple — and less compromising.

Triple sec.

Let the men speak, these criminals, your brothers: they'd act if they didn't speak.

The interpreter and the town crier

Set fair:
Talk to everyone in their hereditary tongue, tell each his own truth (to be translated across all temperaments), this is how God, if he were less clumsy, could establish unity in his work — one dictator, European peace.

Unsettled:
On the contrary, the way to achieve general dissent: speak to everyone using the same words. Misunderstanding will miraculously spread. Multiplication of sects. Heresies guaranteed. (Verified.)

Let others act!
With simple words, it's so easy to be defeated.

Wrong way

At these borders I loiter uncertain of the language of flowers...
(Her mouth has taken on the fold of a lily petal.)
By the longest? By the shortest?... I hesitate, and time passes... passes and goes by again. I leave, rushing my goodbyes. I register my heart. I deposit my fear.

(All roads lead to Rome.)

Walking backwards.

Should an angel do me the honor of undressing themself, unmasking themself in front of me, I'm afraid of embarrassing them, I turn my head or lower my eyes...

Handshake.

A man overboard! A bit of flesh floats, an arm already shattered by refraction, a clenched flower strains, a little frog's foot...

In the lifeboat, the master swimmer (role created by a woman) plays heads or tails with his lead medal... Bah! You can always be polite, it doesn't commit you to anything. He's a shy one, he won't insist; I know him. So long as the tone is right, of course: "How are you, dear friend?"

You can't think of everything.

Placed at the foot of the bed I realize it would be necessary to peel my dress off — and that my skin would come off with it.

Choke pear.[122]

You'd have to burden yourself with theory, know how to handle a flesh toy...

"Squeeze the rubber animal: he gives out a faint cry."

... These instructions fail to take pain into consideration (the patient's feelings). I would be wrong to comply with it.

Useless precaution.

Death — love[123] — it was to be expected. In my mind and with my actual hands, I had already done the preparatory exercises, maneuvers, dress rehearsal. But I hadn't anticipated so many props, criminal refinement, vain formulas, this luxury of adjectives, prefixes, endings, this interminable conjugation of verbs, these days, these garrulous nights, this licentiousness of God's style — the Chinese torturer — boredom — the kiss in the ear.

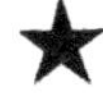

Reparation

(He certainly owes me that.)

It's simple: he knows everything about me that he wanted to. Why should he come back? It would be a waste of time.

In vain I sought, examined each ridiculous argument in turn, each supplication, literary or desperate appeal — no way to attract him, no lie; even insults...

If only I could send my seconds to him, get a duel arranged. At least I'd see him again...

Men are so lucky!

Shuffle the cards.

Masculine? Feminine? It depends on the situation. Neuter is the only gender that always suits me.[124] If it existed in our language, no one would be able to see my thought's vacillations. I'd be a worker bee for good.

The arrangements of the poet with his infirmity

Blind oneself in order to see better. Make sparks fly while striking at shadows. Strike at the deafening silence to make oneself a malleable friend. Strike a mighty blow at syntax and rhythm and the verb to extract from them the water of death.[125]

Unassailable.
He's holding on. But doesn't unassailable equate to indefensible?

The exception proves the rule — and disproves it too.[126]

I'm obsessed with the exception. I see it as bigger than nature. It's all I see. The rule interests me only for its leftovers with which I make my swill. This is how I deliberately downgrade myself. So much the worse for me.

Yet I am obsessed with order. I like to challenge mystery, submit it to reason. I hate preconceptions; but only others'. If I neglect the facts that annoy me, if I pretend to scorn life, it's because the unreal permits one to take all kinds of liberties.

The abstract, the absolute, the absurd, are a malleable element, a plastic material, the word one appropriates. That I reclaim for myself.

And so, at ease, I associate, dissociate — and formulate without laughing the odious rule of my collection of exceptions.

VIII

N. O. N.

It's not enough to be vanquished,
you also have to know how to turn
defeat to your advantage.

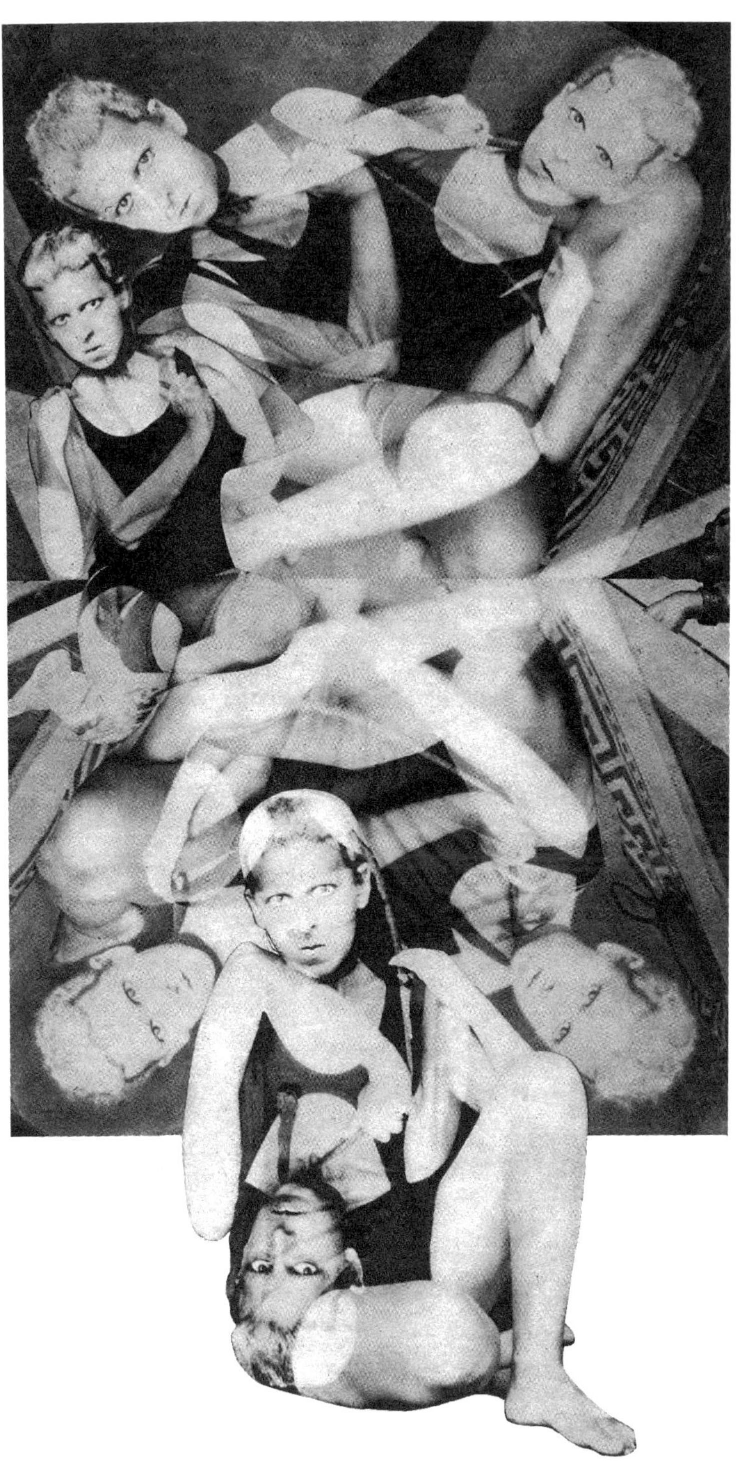

What's the point?

There's no reason to be proud: Even the most honest among us,
— unless handing out pamphlets — all, merchants in the temple.

Beauty products.
Fragile – With Care – Perishable goods.

And even our victories are only ever mutilated victories.

Modesty.
The black crowd, the anonymous: the silvering behind the glass
where the poet admires himself.

Jealousy:

He was afraid of his peers and only spent time with the dead.
But the dead gave him bad advice.

At sea level.

Standing at the edge of the great smooth soul — calmed crowd
— he selected a flat body, the type that make the furthest leaps when
skimmed.

The anachronism of the great puzzle.

With the new timetables, there's no longer any way to look for
midday at fourteen hundred hours. In our utilitarian world, no playing of games is tolerated. It's not such-and-such an artist, but *a
priori* to art itself that posterity does justice in advance.

(It can be put in overalls, nothing will be changed by doing so.)

Not an angel's tail...

Only dry ideas that are isolated, one of a kind, can be easily retained. When an idea falls from running water into a complex realm,
it is lost. I will never rediscover even one letter of it, the initial.

Good will (imperative or conditional).

Try to understand a situation by replacing it with another (if
possible one of ours) — in the same way that you might change a
pronoun in a sentence to work out if you need to use the verb in the
indicative or the subjunctive.

Pro domo[127]

One couldn't be more naive. Great liar and poet, he denounces the concern to be sincere in the name of art: "It's the sign of a sterile genius."

His little sister, who is getting fat, is condemned (or as they say, condemns herself) to prove that beauty, health, virtue are only to be found among women and "sturdy" races.

You could quite truthfully say that we are all born guilty. And we drink to forget. We drink our soul. Drunk but terrified by our little differences, we are obliged to convince everyone else that the truth for everyone is our way of being.

Everyone wants their formula to be the only hope of salvation. Happy boys only take kindly to lightness, a free and easy manner. The afflicted, the rebellious (am I not numbered amongst you?) — we demand dreams, claws out or velvet paws. A philosopher draws up a list of his negative and positive qualities. These will be the new sins, universal values. In the end, for the skeptics, for the believers (be it in God or the devils), to doubt is as to believe.

We know all too well unfortunately that it's they who say this.

Malice stitched with a vulgar thread. Ariane dreams of her little profits.[128] She rigged her labyrinth and I started to distrust the night, the day and the sought-after danger.

I fan my cards in my hand. I show how I value them in the way that I use them. I lose, I win, it's your business. — And it will have been pointless my discussing the king and queen with you... You know this is about mine.

Even if I don't know how to hide my game, will I at least know how to cheat with my cards on the table?

Pass!

They need a password. Even if I had the knack for it, I refuse to summarize the world in five letters — even if it's five capitals. I will no longer resign myself to seeing impurity reduced to five senses, to the seventh art, to the twentieth century. I don't want to know your formula: my memory, tempted by wild strawberries or the werewolf's mouth, would leave it by the wayside. I would approach your sentries already condemned to death. Am I eternal, sluggish and sinking in the sands to sustain you or me with mortal puns? I will desert your armies. I will freely circulate in the intermediate space. We'll see if your gods or your bullets can drive me out of it.

Luxury industries

The great question is not: Does it have a purpose? — but: Does it add anything?

Today Mecenius, if he is not a great business man, is someone who's gone down in the world and is worthy of contempt.[129] What would it matter that Mallarmé's poems are obscure if they could serve to advertise a mask shop or menstrual undergarments? Do you wish to be respected in your lifetime? Take something better to your boss than tentative "hopes"; take him his clientele, ready-made, first sell chestnuts or chips. Vindicated by your profits, you are unassailable ("Since this sells...").

Provided that it is listed on the stock market, the useless beautiful work has pride of place next to the vile work. The wonder of expensive illuminations, the lofty fireworks, so much wasted carbon and so many dazzled eyes (provided that Citroën gets something out of it) do not surprise those — poets! — who protest the most vehemently against the poet's pointless short outing.

Sometimes we are asked to accept that what matters is the most nourishing dish rather than the useless ornaments that decorate the table. But it's just a manner of speaking.

The least nourishing dish and also the least fresh flowers matter very much, where such a combination leads to sales, provided that the people who are paying can be persuaded that certain luxuries are indispensable or that indigestion is the height of happiness.

Supply determines demand. Luxury goods in series become absolutely essential items.

Prostitutes certainly have a lovely line of business. (Maybe there is also room for virtue...) But woe betide the girl who is mad about her body, mad about her soul, who claims she gives her favors just to please herself, pain and pleasures for free! Love for love's sake is disgusting. That is a luxury indeed, the only one described as shameful.

He chose the virtue he found the easiest...

Sell your soul? If you only had to sign it away, it would be quickly done. Faint-hearted when considering an action, the same person is full of daring the very next instant — when impulse closes every door, save the one where our footsteps have already trampled the threshold.

Thankfully, there are still formalities to conclude, the miserly business of bidding. "Simplify your administration, O Satan!" advises a virtuous maiden as she puts herself forward to be damned. There's even more protocol here than in paradise! Where to find one's catechism? Secret protocol: matter of doctrine.

Ivory tower.

(It still exists. It's good to know that it's ridiculous in name only. In reality it's tragic. It's a state institution: a prison for weaklings.)

As soon as I come out of my reverie and dream of making my entrance in the world, I hear doors slam shut.

He is with the age of compromise.

Your madness, your ideal, your soul — what are they worth? It's not vanity but profit that you should be getting from them. Keeping these trinkets at home is greedy; increase them, corner the market; make alms of them, a guilty extravagance.

No one's asking you for the moon. Quite the opposite. We'll all be satisfied if it goes on a secondhand stall. Monuments of piety, that's what we are. Enter into our motives, you are intangible.

Useless precautions.

Whenever my sense of unfinished duty, whenever my weak wish for power, dressed me up as a demon, as a hero all the better to ridicule itself: I was thinking, rather a stain than death! (Otherwise trust in attenuating circumstances.)

Some gloves — gloves' fingers...

A diving suit.

A mask for protection against gas (overly personal odors or suffocating perfumes).

... And then, turning the head away a little...

No guarantee of God.

It's the white soul slave trade, God trafficking his glory...

Vacant position

THEM (Angel's voice):

The torch? Are you insured against fire then?

Are you soaked in the waters of the river Lethe that you deliver your body up for women to bite?

In order to hold the vulgar in contempt, or sometimes to combat it, do you believe yourself to be loaded with fists like a Hindu idol, with innumerable arms and souls — do you think you're the strongest?

Alone with your dishonor which in vain you name your pride, islet battered by doubts and riots (waves unleashed by your own madness), cemetery invaded by ryegrass[130] which you refuse to tear up or which you even sow along with the good grain, alone — are you so sure that you love yourself, sure that you can be enough for yourself?

Alone — which you call: being free, you who forge the bars of your own prison.

Misfortune, hope which will sulk like a chastised child, the vanity of the passions' voluntary exile — for not having conceded the easy concession — and untimely death, this is what the spirit that rejects the recognized rules will meet on its walled-up way.

Stick to the well-behaved, necessary boundary marks of a well-brought-up way of thinking — and you will be saved.

We will give you success, wealth — maybe power. We will ask very little of you in exchange; nothing more than the appearance of capitulation.

Castrate your ill feelings — or even better (a word in your ear) keep them for yourself, secret, decent: put a little loincloth on them...

See how much more accommodating we are than your master. Would he be satisfied with a pretend evil spirit?

We pay in ready cash, just like and better than him; and we ask for nothing in return, just a bit of hypocrisy...

ME — Have I come to this?... So what! I won't succumb. I won't deny my defeat any more than a victory. It's not for loan, nor rent, nor sale. On earth as in hell we are sheltered from vertigo. The demon is not tempted.

Noblesse oblige: Sell your soul to God, truthfully! — impossible downfall for a disciple of the Other.

Dangerous for whom? Do you think I run after the clientele? If the Devil is fencing spices, he's too fond of them himself, he's not making any money out of them. He's eating his capital, he's putting his own ruin first. That he should have left an apple on the tree for Eve is somewhat surprising.

Colors.

Red, the sexual instinct. Yellow, hunger. Blue, fear. And their derivatives: Orange, sociability. Green, tricks. Indigo, consciousness of myself, of humanity. Violet, consciousness of oneself, of the superhuman.

To put it another way: Violet, pride. Indigo, true love. Blue, weaknesses. Green, compulsive lying. Parsimony and avarice, yellow. Orange, vanity. Red, lust and sex mania.

And their corresponding colors on the other side of the prism: Red, courage. Orange, emulation. Yellow, order and energy. Green, art. Blue, goodness, all kinds of indulgence. Indigo, heroism. Violet, dignity — and spirituality.

But I've had enough of tracing the nuances from white to black of the infinite detail of these elastic virtues. Aren't we ever going to discover ultraviolet sentiments? Who wouldn't devote themselves to infrared itself in order to experience the least inaccessible of so many forbidden notes on this incredible, inhuman scale...

The madman

Blind people should be told about colors, deaf people should be shown the vibration of sounds, and we should dance in front of the paralyzed person's coffin — on our feet, on our hands, dance with the whole body...

Angels have had enough of duty, of the happiness of exercising their wings. May they do without my praises! May the birds not expect any speeches about aviation from me.

I want to scandalize the innocent, the little children, the old folks, with my nudity, my raucous voice, the obvious reflex of desire. Those who are without sin, it is good that they cast stones at me, that in my human stupidity (that is to say immortal), the superhuman feels humiliated.

In an indulgent mirror, God smiles at his mouth while he puts his lipstick on... I enter. Get in the middle. He will never again forget that Medusa herself was made in his own image.

Confused in the midst of the invisible, you all — unbelievers — walk straight through me, without wounding yourselves, without realizing.

This is how it is: this futile cruelty, misunderstood, it finds its just desserts in men's scorn.

Who can feel the movement of the earth? It doesn't mean it's turning any the less. Can it stop itself?

If our love is like that, it means we have to roll the rock, fill the barrel, give life to all powers beyond good and evil, all forms without souls, lend our voice, our tongue, our lips, to those who are silent: mute — modest — or dead.

Check the bill.

St. Thomas wants Jesus to start the miracle all over again, for he is one of those who are never completely sure that they've turned off the gas.

The autonomy of the ring finger.

For me, a miracle, terror or charm, surprise, is anything I cannot obtain from my body or soul. For the Christ, the Christ is completely normal. He didn't even get any joy from walking on water.

Fortune tellers.

At the edge of the present, leaning over an abyss... Of coffee grounds or any old washing-up water. Objects placed behind us are reflected clearly in it. We find this reassuring: the whole adventure takes place on the battlefield. The future is under history's guarantee. All's well that ends well.

The eve of battle.

The Orient parades... crouching, trembling, ready to pounce. The Occident's great vigil.

You can always sing or pray while waiting for the executioners — or bite your nails with impatience.

Some prefer to busy themselves breaking spears for their condemned beauty. I pity them. They will never know their role as victim.

Tooth-pullers (amateurs and professionals).

Surgeons are well-intentioned executioners. The difference goes, according to the case, to the people, from scorn to respect, from hatred to love. See it any way you like.

For me, woman I am, and glory in it fleetingly. If someone steps on my toe, let him either love me or apologize.

Artists, false prophets, ponderous intellectuals, etc., are leading the dance because of the mistakes of others, strong people who are so at ease in their skin that they sleep in it and allow themselves to be dominated by us, the weak, the sick, men of the very worst lineage.

One foot in sin, in the tomb, in the abyss. Singe your soul. Approach evil and God to speak out. Bemoan grace. But hold onto the edge, say nothing.

Everyone carries the weight of their own virtues. I cannot commit someone else's sins. I burden myself with them fruitlessly, offer myself to the holocaust,[131] through a martyr's or an actor's vanity prolong my role as others' replicas, in rebellions that are those of my fellow human beings, that are not mine, if I — consciously — try to modify my being, make it more acceptable, my most vile crimes will be considered virtues, somewhere, in God's empty heaven.

Über alles[132]

A Sunday like all the other Sundays outside the world: with no beginning or end. Yesterday it was the creation, around the clock-face in 12 hours, on the hour, on the minute. A circular madness, incessant seconds. This evening: unlimited free time, eternity in slow motion. Necessarily, it's always the same thing.

My eternal enemy hides his cards from the Invisible. — By dint of cheating at the metaphysical game, haven't we acquired that infernal impudence which allows us to see over the shoulder of the Highest Being?

A hand in close-up, fleshy, pink, smooth — simply: naked — and with no heart line. A fan of peoples, churches, erections. Multiform anthills. Majorities assert themselves: quantity and capital. Shadowy capital cities, where the works department, guaranteed by the government is locked behind offensive walls. A cannon stoppering up the holes, dreams with no range, redundant arrow slits... In the work, the race can be perceived, its ideal, its whore, and even the make of the human machine. Red, black, white — and yellow. Occident, Orient, flow into each other like colors or blood that can't congeal. — Cubes, wedding cakes 36 tiers high, 40,000 candles. Beauties with large regular features. — Architecture in a crinoline, pearl gray and royal blue, tradition eliminated, remade, "smart and simple" frills and flounces at the Samaritaine department store, this is

Paris. — Ivy, flower and cabbage patches, mist, pleasure well defended, well kept, discreet glass houses, granite prisons..., etc..., etc...

The imbecile, he's going to carry out an act of God, decide no matter what. Everything will be all right in the end. — No! no, this is the big one. Lay your cards on the table, Lord!

Hasty generalizations

> Children today fear only one thing:
> that their dreams will come true.

Man intervenes with all his weight, seeking a fulcrum on the stone he condemns — diverted law, gravity — pushing apart, bringing down the twin pillars of the temple...

(Happy ruin, impressive ideal, certain success.) No doubt a noble gesture — especially since we saw that he was the first to waver. But the drunken strength of Samson has become scientific. His blows, well calculated. Charlot[133] staggering (because that's still the tradition after all!), but thanks to studio special effects easily escapes the worst and extricates himself unscathed. He can be reborn from our ashes; he has paid the phoenix interest in gold and blood. If someone threatens him with a fine: "I don't care," he says, "I am insured." — All the same he'll collapse under the avalanche he provokes, under outdated theater decorations, will we be grateful to him for his intentions, for sacrificing innocent lives at the same time and more cruelly than his own? Will we avoid criticizing his work? Calling him to account: inventories of deathbeds, review of souls? I can hear his proclamation clearly: Peoples — historians — woman — O mean-spirited sister! I only want to see the necessity of the disaster. Isn't the very ugliness of the rubble my justification? Don't go into detail.

Then in the harsh lights of the fire, a long-haired, indignant shadow makes three slow circuits of the world; assails, surrounds, mounts an assault on the destroyer; stands up to him, draws himself up, dominates him; No prison cell for him, no oubliette.[134] He can be visited. The hecatomb[135] is open to the winds, admirable in itself, with no ultimate excuse. "Always the same ones! And as for creation, didn't you change it long ago for some reason?... You don't understand a thing about it. I am a stone breaker."

Fishers in murky waters

It goes without saying that a pond after a storm is the perfect playground for a poet. Each holds on to his interest by its slippery tail.[136] And the highest interest doesn't have its noble titles any less falsified than the lowest.

My line is well baited. It's quick to work. A few minutes' sunlight will be enough for me. The rest of the time the sky can do its worst. Perpetual rage. Cruelty with no remission (except for the necessary deglutition[137] of blood, and sometimes love at first sight prolonging an erection). I'll lend it a helping hand. — One — two — three. Multiplication of hands. O miracle! Abandon. Relieved passions open their revolting lock gates...

What honest look does not prefer the hour of clarity, the decor in flat tones? Even if it is self-defeating and ends with only one's own face to be seen in them. Monotonous mirage...

— In short, what do you do for a living?

— I resist temptation.

Foresight.

Live in bed, float on your back, so as not to sink in the flood that God certainly owes us this century.

Game of chance.

The Earth spins like a crazy roulette ball. God's forgotten how to cheat. When you look at it, since creation God's come out of this perilous adventure pretty well.

But... Leave while you're winning, O Lord, it's time!

The year 2000 (end of the world).

Does God count the days and strike them off on the Prussian soldier's calendar? Or the Cossack's or the Greek infantryman's?

— On the day, at the time you wish!

— Man, is it up to you to set the rendezvous? Be sure that the Eternal will fall on top of you when your soul is least prepared. Taken by surprise you'll have to improvise your own defense. Don't trust suns, moons, stars — or even spasmodic comets. Your almanac is obsolete.

Balance is our law.

In creating matter, God decreed a certain part of the soul as a dowry for himself. But too many bodies nowadays fight over the legacy.

Tin of sardines (democracy).

There should be more games going on in human relationships. Ideas barge into each other, passions collide, our souls — like sheep — are rammed on top of each other now that millions who willingly got themselves crucified have stopped showing off about their suffering, dropping the "de" in their names, burning their noble letters and shouting: "Every man for himself!"

Science thickens, the air is gluey, the blood sticks in our veins. The density of by-products immobilizes art itself. Crabs vomit our waste. The ocean is decomposing.[138] — Catastrophes and blonde beauties are served.

It's a soup the spoon can stand up in.

Each century (century is not exactly the right word here), every arbitrary fraction of time, ushers in a moralist with his own new morality. This can never be just once and for all. The slightest change of morals involves a shift of focus.

There are some basic tasks that have to be seen to each and every day.

Depopulation.

I will give the same explanation for pain (since I don't believe in it any longer) as others have given for pleasure. The same theory, summed up by the optimist and the pessimist:

Pleasure: lure for reproduction.

Pain: obstacle to reproduction.

A chicken lays an egg and sings. A woman lies down, is as good as dead for a few days, and groans. Why this difference? The race of chicks is a good race; there will never be too many of them in the world, especially since we love them *ab ovo*.[139]

The children of men are harmful for the most part. It is claimed that they are edible... But if they've been devoured a long time before their birth, it's best not to brag about it. Besides, whatever you do, there are too many of them, they're dirty and they take up space...

In short, God noticed that the world is soiled, that his garden is littered with greasy wrappers from ink, sweat and gold (yes, I do maintain that gold is greasy).

— Reduce their number. Through some excess, naturally. I would have suggested excess of well-being... but since Luther and Calvin, who could boast of having converted God? Not even the beautiful foliage of sterile fig trees was able to touch his heart...

He makes wars, disasters, suffering, etc. forcibly intervene...

What has man got to moan about when he has consigned himself to the prompter's hidey-hole?

Parasite
(without committing oneself)

Modesty! Mite of invisible adventures, of discreet transformations, the corpse's flirtation, sully the murderer's hand with gold, perforate time, avarice, pierce holes in stockings... Here am I, innocent, a jobless virgin, a queen on strike, voluntarily unemployed, marginalized and as they say, outlawed from society.

Follow my example: Stay at home and eat wool.

Moldy patches

Here I am. I've been put against the wall in penitence. Shall I measure its thickness, calculate its length and breadth, multiply, count how many stones high it is?... Leave these jobs to others. Let me have the best bit. I can do nothing other than dream when faced with its noble blemishes, moldy patches where each finds the form of his loves, loses it, finds it again and can then see nothing else (surprised by surprised looks, shame, angry that the whole world can't see it too) until the day when he himself... An imperceptible displacement of the soul has clouded the mystery. The man had confused the image with his own superimposition.

Mutable monsters (what am I saying?), decor where the god's skin sticks, where his dark sweat drips, poignant imprint, unique, irrefutable fingerprint evidence.

A love potion of glory
(poison for external use)

Illustrious men assert that they have read, reread and augmented the lives of their fellows in Plutarch.[140] They have always been careful to avoid having a twitch, the anecdotal, the peculiarities of genius — traps that commentators willfully proffer them. They know that they'll always produce enough of their own.

What to say of the willing failure, who out of disgust for common measures, vulgar virtues, seeks abandonment, deliberately takes on all the "if onlys" of Fortune?

Lover of weaknesses, do you think you'll make a good stock of love by boiling up the lovers' chastity belt, their breakup letters, their crocodile tears and purple sage?

Add the playthings of your solitary nights, and serve cold.

False value
(virgin gold)

Pride, so far as I can make out, consists of establishing that our unrefined riches (even given that the veins are very poor) weigh more than the minted riches of this world's great ones.

It's all about reducing things! Exchange rates, generations of bankers, mean little to me. Let the Bank of France either buy back my gold or prohibit it, it's its own business. But so long as the ore is taken from the mine and the metal extracted according to all the rules of art, I will not allow myself to forget it.

Scruples (my defense).

I am frightened of misinterpretations. If I omit the slightest inflection, I distort the verb and the whole of life. It's much better to show only the tiniest corner of it.

Them — That's quickly said!

Me — It would take me too long to say.

The iris that I cannot put makeup on.

Memory? Selected extracts. My soul is fragmented. Between birth and death, good and evil, between the tenses of the verb, my body serves me in transit.

196 —

The breach.

Just as we are about to extricate ourselves from the game, swept away by the intellectual rapids, derail, escape from the infernal circle — tangential, unconscious, haggard, half-ghosts — suddenly, with a jerk, the body clings back on. Scenes. Crisis. The monotony of its ticketed, timed caprices, its old girl's obsessions and worse, its animal appetites, must be suppressed.

I get in my shadow's way quite horribly and can't escape it: we've been handcuffed.

Keep an eye on your sleep.

The musician, the painter, are the true civil servants of the absolute. Once they've done what they have to, they can pack up their bags. Obviously when it comes to the ear and the eye, they never stop working. But it is not enough for a writer to put an arm in the machine; he has to get in completely. If he holds anything back, the diamond will be spoiled by such a blemish that all the world's brilliance will be in vain.

Watch out for alternatives!

The poet has to sacrifice himself twice: for himself and for the other. (Sentence needs rewriting.)

The poet has to be ready to sacrifice his life twice:

For the love of art — his work, posterity, the king of Prussia...[141] But when it comes down to it he's a man like everyone else: for you, for himself, for the first to arrive.

— However, I am no less cowardly about it!

Formal notice.

Marsyas[142] is a myth for little children only. Play with the flayed one[143] and don't overindulge your skin.

Dying of hunger

Before I get there, how many dead people will I meet on my way that I won't know how to avoid. Before corporeal privations, only futile privations: love, ambition, liberty, harmony, dream... The least chimeric Roman is as likely as a Russian to allow the circus to take precedence over daily bread.[144]

If I regain consciousness after so much fainting, I will suffer unspeakable discomforts in my flesh which is devoted to so many more delicate torments; finally cold, weakness... and insomnia will make all food disgusting to me. Everyone carries unexpected conclusions within themselves, among these, to face up to the great fear, the great desire must not be forgotten.

But under another name: vertigo, aren't they inseparable?

Mysterious without makeup, we touch her with a finger. Play bones with a skeleton.[145] (I recommend it to all barefoot children at Christmas, without a nest for eggs to be laid in.)

We've got the beautiful praying mantis who devours those she has fiercely fascinated within our skins, bone deep, and that isn't all. We desire her less than we respect her. We are interested in her soul more than anything. In her rest.

The dead get ready

I thought we had a definite rendezvous that day, I'd dressed up for her[146] down to the finest detail. Eyelids closed on this world of vanities, my lips uniting in a kiss of peace, my right and left finally reconciled, I waited for her. But she's not very punctual.

Thrice I redid my preparations, thinking each time to put less hope into it, more negligence, but conceding to my taste for the ostentatious.

Is it the unexpected that she requires? Make a soul of myself in order to please her?

Well, let her leave me! — or take me as I am.

Death without sentences.

Death = Simplicity. Once and for all.
Life = Complexities. Always having to start again.

Life, demanding wife to be reconquered beside each bed. Daily bread. Work or unemployment.

No one spends much on a girl who's just passing through. You don't experience much shame with someone there's no risk of seeing again.

Uncertainty still keeps us from our goal. But we would be wrong to encumber ourselves with an arms license, a flask or instructions. The end will soon have justified the worst chosen means.

With neither flowers nor crowns.
Thanks to God, and despite our pretensions, we scarcely dream about, scarcely think about death.

Good little chickens, innocent fattened calves, pigs led to abattoirs, blindfolded like love.

Success has crowned our efforts. But with a crown of thorns.

No letters this morning? Fine, it's for the best!

I have a lot of luck. But unpleasant, negative. It consists of putting the privative "a" in front of all dangerous, unhealthy or simply dubious pleasures. I have a taste for pleasure, questionable ambitions...

But your, our covetousness taken as a whole, and humanity itself, aren't all these unreliable?
My luck, after all, would only be a sophism.
— It's always like that.

While waiting for words to cross swords, I want to be a second for them.

Before the cock crows I will deny myself without counting.

The defenseless animal: feigns death. In the same way my soul rolls itself up into a ball, my pride contracts, my life draws its claws back in all the way up to its armpits, to the groin. Up to the neck, in shadows sinking. All who have a shell gather up their vulnerable desires and put themselves in solitary confinement.

While I was still young and supple, I began these laudable practices. I became so used to doing them that I wouldn't know how to sleep unshielded. But as soon as the eye was under the tortoise,[147] I dreamed only of denials:

Fearing that he isn't expecting to inherit from me and doesn't care for my body, I surrender my soul to God in advance.

To avoid making anyone jealous:

Fearing that he will lead me into seeking adventure, Marguerite or Titine,[148] or any other conventional happiness — and to have some peace — I bequeath my portion of paradise to the demon.

Let them sort it out!

Conflicting renunciations. — I am signing both registers at once, but without conviction. Imitating my own handwriting. Will I be convicted of fraud? — Eternity, a futile threat! At the call for immortal souls, what will be done about the one hidden under earth who hasn't moved?

The eternal return

Like the sea — like history — the gods are tireless.

When Eurydice died for the second time,[149] the gods, moved by Orpheus' fury, promised him a second proof.[150]

"Enough of this recidivism!" the poet replied. "You're not going to make me entrust my weathercock to the thousand winds or imitate the squirrel in its cage for nothing any longer. I accept the blindfold, I reject Eurydice. Certainly, it will be easy for me to blind myself, to shut my eyes to the past if, instead of Eurydice, I bring Beatrice back from the Inferno.[151] A new life. It doesn't matter who I love and who I need and if I lose on the deal. I won't pay a widow's mite for another go on the merry-go-round. Substituting one object with the same object is fine for you, the immovable.

"If someone steals my handkerchief, I'll cry all the tears of a head cold in vain, blowing my nose in any fresh sock whatsoever rather than buy another one just the same. At least I will have the feeling of being alive, of perfecting my pain, of adding another string to my lyre.

"Orpheus doesn't join the circle. That's a game for children, slaves and submissive stars."

Absolutes

Difficult children, that's what we are. The earthly paradise of the Bible would never be enough for us. Far from it. Even Muhammad's self-improvements scarcely touch us except on café terraces. Swept along by time, women seem really insipid to us. We have learned to twist sacred sentiments like the licorice bars of a prison for a laugh. Cinema contributes to the perversion of our supra-celestial ambitions. Allusions, ever clearer, to pleasures outside nature (an elastic body in a plastic landscape). Our hair stands on end and it's already getting its claws from space and time. We need original miracles, supernatural content according to the latest fashion.

Adam attacks God, Eve her man, the Creator his accomplice... But the serpent chucked the apple on the dunghill himself: "It's over-ripe," he said.

Nauseated by Christ, Jesus refuses communion: a gamy host.

"Fall in!"

In the sunlight, the shadow is clearly defined. Alone and dense, it draws itself up, stretches out and slowly turns.

But in our shattered night, the faceted stars cling to windows, to the fastest bursts, to overwhelming moments. A spume of colors and fires flickers under our eyelids, dazzling the twilight, disintegrating the darkness, multiplying our double, rendering it too familiar. We can't take a step without walking over us, circled by our shadows as we are, attacked by our shadows, of varying thicknesses and weights, thrashing about, shoving into each other and leaping at our throats.

Someone, it doesn't matter who, it doesn't matter which of these madwomen it was, squared up to me, threw me to the ground and took my place. In vain. The game begins again, the same infernal game, of shadow in its turn deceived, of scattered flesh that the head lamp of a car sweeps up, of fugitive gestures that an electric light renders formless, of an influx, of a reflux of reflexes whose blindfold can be lifted by the slightest vibration of light.

May it come at last, the magnet, the catalysis, the shadowy beauty, always effective and never corroded. May he come, he who does not go from door to door proclaiming his power, he who will enter my body without knocking... Let him come!

After him, strong from him, all I will have to do is appear.

Is it "catalyst" rather than "catalysis"? It sounds wrong somehow.

IX

I. O. U.

We get the god we deserve, unfortunately for us.

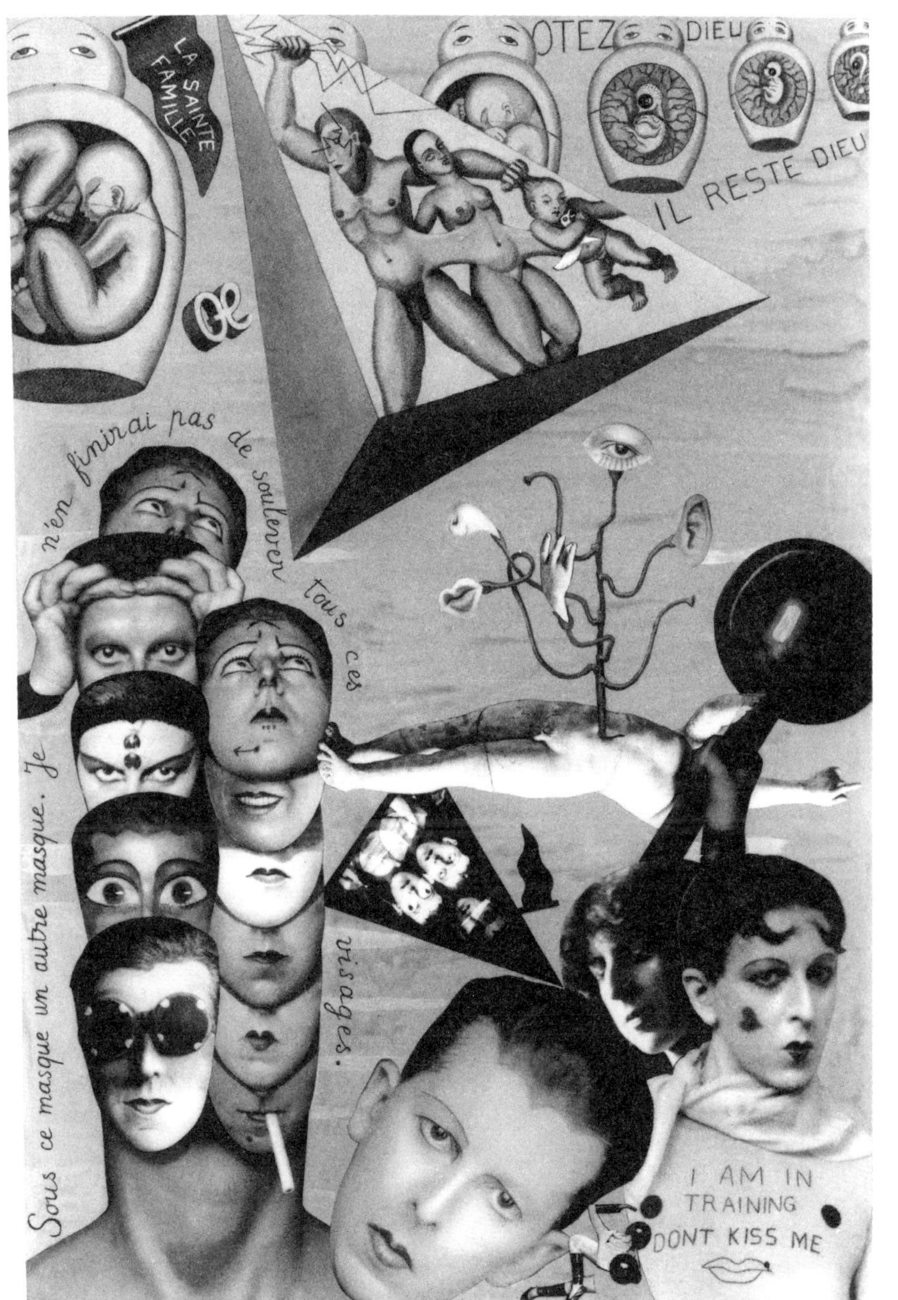
LA SAINTE FAMILLE
OTEZ DIEU
IL RESTE DIEU
n'en finirai pas de soulever tous ces
Sous ce masque un autre masque. Je
visages.
I AM IN
TRAINING
DONT KISS ME

I OWE YOU

Pray while yawning — but pray!

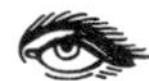

Metaphysical cowardice.

You've had enough of the sky above your head, and the wind of vertigo bends your knees. In such a state, you don't give a damn about truth, about the earth... It is enough to reassure you that the lookout calls from the crow's nest: Horizon!

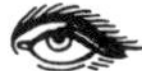

Earth to earth.

Purgatory is within our reach: only uncertainty is human. Paradise without the fear of leaving it is equal to hell without hope. A sensual pleasure only exists to the extent one is threatened with losing it.

They only appreciate their happiness in retrospect. Up above, if they haven't changed soul, they'll be retelling the same little tales about their lives down here like so many old women. They'll be saying: Those were the good old days!

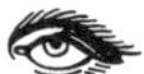

God.

I sometimes speak about what is true, more often about what is false. How can you distinguish them?

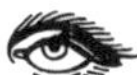

Behind each deed lies faith. I don't care which, I just need one. Without it, everything denies itself, silences itself, mouths eat their words. Destruction itself waits in suspense. My hair, my nails stop growing. The dead surely have some obscure belief.

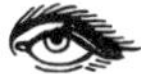

I am in training, don't kiss me.

If ever it happens that I believe in a god outside myself, at certain times it seems to me that he has got the upper hand: having eternity before him. With those means at their disposal, any murderer, innocent, prostitute, the bottom of their class, the lowest of men, could equal him, could easily topple him from his throne... Yes, saved from the intolerable distractions of poverty, love, illnesses, and at the same time, allowed to take my time, I'd feel like his equal...

And maybe he wouldn't be much of a match for me, who knows?

Self-development.

I would never wish to worry myself, burden myself with anything else. Alas! We can only chase that hare by pursuing all the others at the same time.[152]

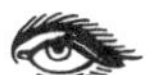

Litmus paper

We should mistrust the blue reactions of the soul. If it's easier to agree on negations, that doesn't lead very far. The enemies of our enemies are not our friends.

It would be better to admit that all beings are, in one way or another, incompatible. This doesn't prevent negotiation, nor even the meeting and amalgamation of the powers that you know, living proofs. If the destroyer has his wiles, have no doubt that the creator has his.

I would like to add a sentence but cannot do so out loud. Let each of my adversaries approach: I will whisper it in their ear.

Has God himself ever been able to talk to you otherwise?

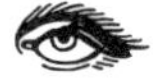

In praise of paradox

Great proverbs are mirror writings, bedsteads, perfect statues. Let's play going around in circles. Each time you come up with a sentence, it would be wise to turn it over to see if it's good. It's easier than casting out the nines.[153]

The nymph Echo, wanting to please Narcissus as much as the fountain, sent his words back to him, face to face and front to back.[154]

The echo, the one that comes from God, returns my thought (subject, interchangeable suffix, verb intact — the verb being the Word.)

The echo, the one that comes from my thought, returns God like a mirror my body (right and left interchangeable — and the middle a good likeness I am told.)

Shouldn't the soul and truth then have their cardinal points?

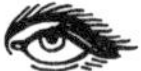

Happiness is not found at bargain prices.

Mistrust pleasures that cost nothing, innocent joys, free passions, compassions and even great heroic repentances on the cheap. Taking everything into account these are the dearest. You'll be left holding the babies, bodies ill from intellectual excesses, the eyes of the blind, exhausted imagination — yes, heart palpitations due to solitary pride — obstetricians, wet nurses, daughters, medicines, taxis, tips and taxes to pay.

If God would only deign to list his rates.

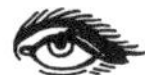

God, dreading that he might succumb to the incestuous, consubstantial temptation to reintegrate man (his work) into his breast, as Sigurd hid behind his sword in order to sleep with the Valkyr,[155] has put painful flesh between him and us.

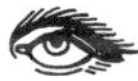

Sentimental education.
The dance of life: the dance of bears on sheets of white-hot metal.
— Without touching it, without touching the victims: their illness is contagious.

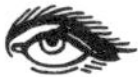

He likes tormenting things. (Put yourself in his place!) He would prefer unbreakable toys. Is death his creation? For replenishing his stock he has not found better. But death does him a disservice. This means of escaping prematurely bothers him more than us.

If we could feel what awaits us when we have invented a way to make ourselves immortal, we would not be so hasty; and far from looking for ways to prolong our lives would rush toward sleep while it was still at the mercy of our eyelids, within reach of our sweet lead bullets.

God's main problem is dosing his poisons skillfully. It requires psychology. How much can this soul take? How much this other? Delicate experiments. Reaching the extreme of human resistance... To have the absolute within and to flounder among approximations. Imprecise limits. To profit from all our possibilities — what patience! Were it not for virtue great vices could never be satisfied. It requires perfect self-control. Sensuality sweeps him along. He is often tempted to go further, like a good guide holds himself back at the edge of pleasure in order to keep his client there. Don't lose your footing, don't cut the rope. That would be dishonorable!

Sometimes the tension is unbearable... But God knows how to preserve good behavior.[156] He resorts to myths, and consoles himself with a symbol (like you or I). Not the same:

Man created paradise — but God's paradise is hell.

Liberal enjoyment of his privileges. Torture at his discretion. His omnipotence finally makes itself felt in the infinite.

Despite such instincts, like a pretty woman, he takes care of his reputation. Reticent in his sadism, he takes care to behave delicately.

Anecdote: A poet does not recognize the right to kill. Is this a reason to allow little fleas all over us? Who will hunt Toto's? There are some souls going cheaply. We'll find one to burden with the necessary sins for a few bucks.

Necessary for what? For our happiness — which probably doesn't leave us in a very good situation, as far from our senses as the pole of logic is from the pole of reality. Nothing is more hypocritical than the truth.

So God hires himself an executioner.

Satan (see Stroheim)[157] willingly plays the villainous roles, the most difficult, rebellious horses. Traitor in love with his mission. Judas selling Jesus for a kiss (he would gladly give you thirty deniers for it), for the beauty of the gesture.

He does evil for evil's sake, honestly, without an ulterior motive, as they used to say not so long ago: art for art's sake.

Free of charge and optional.

Nothing more is required. But what can be used against him? What has ever been used against him? Art for money, bringing in so little; bad business. — Art for reputation (glory or scandal); futile! Am I going to work for peanuts? — Art to corrupt young people? Ah! If it was of any benefit to me... But no. So it's just tyranny! Again no, it's simply so illusory... Change the world? Come on! Will you ever prevent it from changing? Draw your own conclusions.

For myself, I will do as the earth does in turning for the sake of turning, while waiting to discover a good reason.

It only remains for me to send this God that I've made in my image on his way. When he seems like the most vulgar of all my friends, I will allow for attenuating circumstances. All in all, he's more to be pitied than blamed. I wouldn't like to be in his shoes.

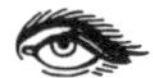

Description

Average forehead
Average eyes
Average intelligence
Sensitivity — not very apparent

Big ears

Expressive lips, flexible tongue

Agile hands, hands of a juggler — for Olympia or pickpocketing

DISTINGUISHING FEATURE: A lifeline running right around the thumb.

On this line of eternity, without beginning or end, where nevertheless whole worlds appear and disappear, the race of seven-day circuits began so long ago that the sun and the moon (referees and runners) have lost count of how many times they've been around the course.

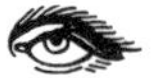

Temptation with a discount
(wide choice of original sins)

Our everyday sister, the contemporary Eve, carves an apple in pork fat:

"It's just as nice at home," she says, — "and cheaper! Serpent, don't you recognize the smell of your crime? Has the blood of Jesus been too effective in washing the trunk of the tree where... ? History is full of new beginnings. Am I not the one — or exactly like the one — the Lord designated for you? What if we play around until the second coming?

"Really? You refuse to make that mistake? You're a snob! You've settled down, domesticated old beast! Old grass snake that asks for nothing more than to stay in his skin!

"Demon! Have a grope of my bosom... You see I'm pregnant with your doings — and you abandon me!..."

Satan: How vulgar! And nowadays they're all like that. Viennese junk.

God (apologizing): What can I do! Psyche seems to please you only. However, I can't work just for you. For fear of being incomprehensible, I've had to go in for some popularization.

214 —

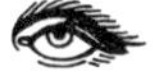

Imitation of the Serpent.

He, furious: I'm going to change skin. You can put the old one on.

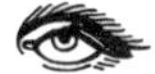

Three against one
(Comic Turns)

Seated in the music hall, and in good seats I hope, you're watching the show. Please! (Wait a little: by dint of electrical switches, a dance of crossing light beams, we'll give you the theater.) They pass around the number 7.

It's Sunday in Paradise. Take care! Eve is in heat. The neighborhood tomcats come running, well-trained, lots of them and in good shape.

The Serpent uncoils a thousand tails, an apple blossom on his lips, — at a jaunty angle — darts his black well-lacquered tongue, makes his irresistible eyes gleam. Waiting for the match to begin, he shadowboxes: he slanders the assorted webfooted fantails (far too hefty! clumsy gait, scruffy feathers), compares his scales to the peacock's colors and bets on himself to win — premeditating rape by cunning.

God, jealous, shows first the tip of his beard then suddenly makes his whole face appear, abandoning the rest to the night. His electric halo rises up, its multicolored rays flash on and off, a garish advertisement and in really bad taste, but, he believes, effective. Projectors. New effect with revolving lights. "The bird with stupid eyes on its feathers has never encountered such clear incitations to spasmodic pleasure... Promise of joy: frequency and variety. Aren't they worth futile beauty?" Cunning tricks! What he's really up to is breaking and entering. Rape by force.

Adam, poor clown, now on his hands, now on his feet, spins his whole body around unadorned. His nudity is his only fortune. All his hopes lie in his rosy ugliness, his obvious weakness and the whims of desire. If only he could cry out to Fortune at the right moment that his wheel is coming unscrewed, pull himself up and... He relies on chance — he dreams of rape by accident.

Eve, O motherland! has put on her best shield: she's doing the splits. She juggles with worlds rolled up into balls, and passes from hand to hand, without pricking her fingers: suns, hedgehogs, moons, fruits, dead stars...

Because of the public, she turns her back on her males who are doggedly pursuing their own stage lights. This business is between rivals. In short, the game is being played out without her... on honeymoon with her own flesh which a hidden demon revealed to her, her veins blue rivers drawn into the sand of her skin, and the swelling of her heart (the most successful of the four displays)...[158]

Her look wavers. Watch out for destiny's clumsiness!

An apple falls in the orchestra pit.

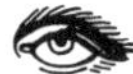

Eternity created this triple-faced monster.

Bouquet of gods. A trinity to tread the boards. Father, mother and son (spirit, heart and body) soldered together by these fleshly arms, these creaking hinges...

And the French family models itself on this.

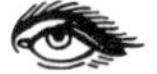

The genesis of Eugenie

Seventh generations,
cross and multiply;
and the children of your children,
through hereditary rights
(that inalienable heritage)
will hand down, and will wear
until the extinction of the centuries,
— and will pass on in turn —
a lily of the valley at the shoulder.

God the Father: "Ah! So that's how it is! You don't want to conceive? You don't want to have a child? But I am the most powerful: I'll create you a daughter who will miscarry in agony every month. You'd like to be celibate, men disgust you? Virgin, you are mad, your daughter will retain just enough sanity to suffer and to damn her mother! Weak people are consoled by words. Woman! Eugenie shall be our child's name!"

And will she bless her father? He hasn't even dreamt of it... It's not predicted in the Holy Scriptures.

Maybe, after all, he doesn't give a damn. He's done his duty as a French man: he's repopulated Cayenne.[159]

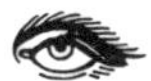

He: You'll pay me for that.
The other: I am insolvent.

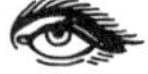

Crowned with a mourning veil and orange blossom, life goes in for some exhibitionism.

Beatific, the animals watch, their heads on one side, wide-eyed. Curses on me, curses on those who look at life badly: either too much or not enough. We will receive the mark of blood that consigns us to contempt, to the axe, sometimes even to death. We will rise again from our wounds and the baptism of our tears will harden our hearts.

But each lunar month, born again in pain, life will take care to revive our enormous frailties, reopen our feelings of disgust, and mix its imperial dignity into our shame.

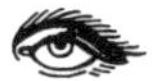

But we can't do anything about it.

Heaven has its roots in hell. Blue roots the image of flames. The most dangerous enemies of good are those who seek to suppress Evil and the evildoer, in the literal, in the figurative sense, who would root it out of the world. If they succeeded (they would have a hard job), it would be a complete deforestation of the highest values. There would no longer be the slightest contrast, everything would lose its balance, pleasure would disappear, and even sleep. Our nights would wither, flowers cut from dreams. Words would be everywhere but never in the right place. Without ugly things, without pain, without opposites, I cannot remain standing.

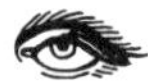

It's a monument: you have to walk around it.

A cat is more curious than you: it puts out its paw, encounters the strange flawless piece of glass, it grates its claw on it, checks the conformity of images — and goes to sniff at the back of the mirror.

The practical man sold Goodness. Good riddance! — Now it's the Antichrist who gets on our nerves. It should be time to nail Evil on the cross of calvary, let him taste the agony of his milk brother.[160] Dispatch them back-to-back.

To save precious wood (tree trunks are expensive this year, carpenters too): I propose that Satan be crucified on the other side of the True Cross.

This new god Janus might bring us the peace of the soul, the wisdom of the spectrum whose colors tolerate each other, the black-and-white flag — without bloodshed.[161]

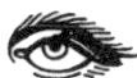

One for all.

Acknowledge the change of ownership — for I cannot perpetually utter my funeral oration.

... It's a question of life and death for the shadow of my steps.

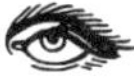

The Heteroclite does not allow itself to be incarnate either in one, or all.

The most insignificant puppet believes that she alone is made in the image of the Virgin Mary. But I've puffed myself up, stretched, padded myself out, made use of my rubbish, all my nail clippings to no avail; can I create nothing more than the world in miniature?

Multiplying himself, God subdivided himself to infinity. In vain do we seek his likeness in the universe. Those who bring us together in their heterogeneous hearts (believing they are reconstituting original unity) are children playing in the dust, old men who know nothing more about their mistress than the texture of her skin.

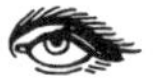

Snowball

A rolling stone gathers no moss, but covers the original form in clay where gravel sticks, debris, so well bound together by the movement, so thoroughly incorporated, that its form is no longer visible, nor its point of origin. The dung beetle's dung ball grows fatter, hardens, suffices to set off an avalanche. Whoever wishes to strip his soul bare must expect to see the dubious amalgam completely fall apart in his hands.

This surgical blade with which analysis or religion arms us against ourselves will it encounter an ivory core — or just rubbish, rubbish, piles of rubbish all the way into its unrecognizable center, dust swept along with the wind?

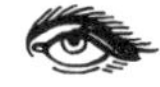

Dispersal

On the day of my baptism, God gave me a box of sugared almonds. To dispose of wholesale or retail. Free to choose consumers as I pleased.

Instructions for use

1st — Decorate with a ribbon, a ticket — and sell.

2nd — Send to the family and relations.

3rd — Keep for oneself to be sucked in secret.

4th — Slip them by force between your lips, end up taking them back from your mouth with my teeth, if the sugar is growing pale, if it's getting smaller too fast; if your pleasure isn't conspicuous enough, if mine isn't sensitive enough. We would never unconditionally hand our souls over to the one who lives near us (we know too well the use he would put them to). It's just a loan. We want guarantees. So we are usurers then, how loathsome. In your place, I would give everything back, demand a receipt and throw this impudent Jew into the street. I'd do it, you have to do it: I demand justice! But I can foresee the consequences and I know my own interests. Whoever you are, my sugared almonds aren't for you, they are not for any one person alone.

5th — Let the greedy and the hungry come to me. Hold the box open. They'll displease me, they'll eat disgustingly, they'll waste them, they'll use me. I will see on their cheek the rose that is my rose, on their hair that I have not chosen the brown of my pralines. The verb "to love" only interests me in the active.

6th — Distribute them among those whom I love. Standing, shivering, on the steps of the church. It's raining. When a beautiful child passes by, I throw a handful of this loose change, white and reddening and bruised. Not only if he passes by, even if I happen to imagine that one day he will maybe pass by... The sugared almonds fall in the mud... Can he debase himself to that? — Puerile faith. Ah! How well I understand his disdain...

But I will continue nevertheless, living, against all odds, to scatter my soul. Remember that you are dust...

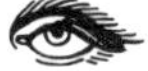

The cracked plate

Angels with patched wings, sails: flirtations, last-minute modesties... Let's use up heaven down to the dregs, the verb down to the insult, the espadrille and the lyre down to the last string. I've had enough of darning, making life last, this putrefaction, this suffering. Survival takes too much effort. Let's go for the fastest done: to the photographer's, to the guillotine, to the brothel, in my arms...

Me, alone at last. Naked haste. Don't hesitate. Don't change your mind. Fall. Doesn't matter where, when, how, only do it. Take yourself at your word.

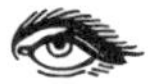

The unsociable one.

At least when one is alone, alone at last, only one enemy remains to be conquered.

— The ultimate marriage of convenience!

Gold or lead, it's too heavy. This heart must be thrown overboard. Between my mirror and my body, shorten the leash.

— And now, onto we two.

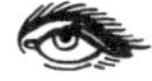

Paper target

Liberated from the ring (this prison, the socket), maybe the eyeball would start to turn... Would move around the sky, people itself with my creatures, adorable world!

He's seen enough of himself. No longer belongs to himself. He's been sent off the rails. The bitterness that tightly bound him to himself has been reduced. No intimacy possible between us. See him absorbed by his new life, caught in the lime of this taste for many realities — transitory, accessory. All concentration lost in the curiosity for knowing, changing the unknowable, unchanging world, in the desire to act (even if only on himself), in the wish to get mixed up in everything. (He who disentangled himself so exclusively from others!) — To become instead of being. He feels alienated. In other words: sold.

He should end it.

Hit full in the face, right in the center of the soul, in the heart of the eye — of the only one that counts (my right eye, since birth, is an unsilvered mirror). Hit the most obvious: right in the heart of the black, dilated pupil. And so as not to miss, in front of the magnifying mirror...

It's nearly done already. All that remains is the cocked end of the finger, the round mouth ready to howl when the bullet leaps forward — and the aim, the prey, the fear, the circle of darkness widening...

For the first time, the beautiful little convex images, the eye's illuminations, the world's innocent miniatures, the feeble representations of space, reflections, have ceased to be. What I see inside: this abominable bleeding hole, comes from time, from myself, from within.

A hand falls back down, limp.

The intensity, the shame, could be enough: if he's not dead he's scarcely better off. The disdained right eye, furious, squirts its invisible ink — and the left eye, renouncing itself, dignity, miracles, finally doesn't dare look at itself in the end.

1928

I want to change skin: tear the old one from me.

REMOVE GOD I REMAIN[162]

Don't go leaning over others, guard
yourself against the call of the abyss...
I might squash someone while falling.

I have spent thirty-three years of my life wishing passion-
ately, blindly, that things would be other than they are. I've acquired
little more than fictional values. I don't know what bill is due today.
But I can feel it. My good side and my bad side, whatever they are,
have to be expressed, with the minimum loss...

Live and grow in me, he she — or simply it — that allowed me,
still young, to understand that I should only, because I can only,
connect with, change, myself.

If the universe is in the mood for metamorphosis, that can only
concern each for himself. No time to lose in bringing about our own
salvation. It behooves the immutable alone to worry about others.
The immutable, that is to say a fossilized soul, a cadaver.

If he wasted any time at all, just one second in his short career,
Jesus damned himself... because he was living.

But who can say whether Christ didn't get himself crucified to
expiate his own mistakes, on his own account, to acquit his own
conscience only.

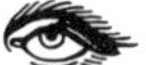

The n... th day God regretted having created Heaven and Earth.

He wanted to destroy his work. But it had fallen into the public domain.

So he descended in himself, divided himself into three to diminish his responsibility, invented the Serpent — and changed pseudonyms.

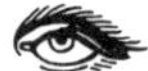

The unnameable

Consciously, unconsciously, whether we squander ourselves, or save ourselves for future generations, if we go to sleep surrounded by precautions, by all possible contempt, if we use ourselves, sperm and blood, sweat and tears, down to the dregs, if we obey ourselves, if we revolt against ourselves or admire ourselves, if we lead ourselves on a leash like a queen, if we feed ourselves like a dog, if we are made of straw or wooden beams, if we see ourselves as beautiful and good, unique or legion, at our pleasure, at our pain, whether we feel abstract or concrete, each treats himself, should and can only treat himself according to his merit.

Make myself another vocabulary, brighten the silvering on the mirror, wink, swindle myself, improve my skeleton with a fluke muscle, correct my faults and copy my actions, divide myself to rule myself, multiply myself so I can make my mark, in short: make a mockery of ourselves — that can't change anything. Anyway, brush me up the wrong way like yesterday and always — no, that doesn't change anything.

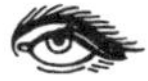

P. S. — A new position for loving myself, for hating myself, a new contact was finally put within reach, at my mercy: An image of the world formed from truths that stick out a mile, a psychology, a morality, painted in *trompe l'âme*.[163] A life-sized religion in papier-mâché, grapes your pigeon would shatter its beak on... Or if you deserve better: a more real order of things (or at least more plausible) than the chaos our senses bear false witness to.

But why hasten toward eternal conclusions? It behooves death, not sleep (another trompe-l'oeil), to conclude. Life's role is to leave me uncompleted, allow me only freeze-frames.

Start again. Connections, repairs, reiterations, incoherence, so what! provided that something else continually comes along. Work essentially obscene and destined to pass through the hands of all viable newborns — however protected or disgusted they are in the crib.

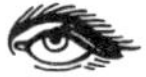

MOI — The one: What a life! It's not mine.
— The other: The intonation is correct. A little more conviction and I'd come to your aid.

Œ — In vain do I try to put my body back where it was (my body with its dependencies), to see myself in the third person. The "I" in me is like the "E" taken into the "O."

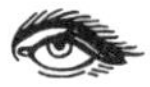

Get out of the O...

A Greek temple far away smokes through its seven columns of factory chimneys — without body, without visible building, sweating the green lawn... The Christian era in ruins returns to the centuries where the years are counted backwards.

Bodies and souls, how skeletons resemble each other! It seems to me that it's the fat, the excess, that are the individual distinctions we're so proud of.

Seven? To count identical objects you have to touch the space. I wouldn't read my rosary of eyes. A letter constantly repeated is a dead letter.

Let's talk about repetitions! — J. H. told me yesterday that I was a squirrel: I nibble a nut, greedy, relaxed. Someone who makes me feel awkward turns up unexpectedly and I nip off. — It's true. Don't push me: you would find out for yourselves.

I stop, foot raised to flee. Flee in a circle. What else can I do in this cage where the squirrel circles furiously. Furiously... and yet yet he circles. He and she. Moon, cage. — This prophet of the Unknown, of the umpteenth true God, has he scientifically discovered the tangent? Can we find at the bottom of ourselves the virtue to escape this horrible cycle? I believe, but in the conditional: I would like to believe.

And while I claim to be seeking to emancipate myself from the machine-like circle of the worlds, thoughts made in series, word games and crazy images... the root of the third statue turns slightly blue to join the vein in my temple for evermore.

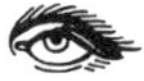

I'll do whatever is required for this and it'll turn out well...

One fine day he is before me. And me: "When will he come?" — "It's him!" It's not him. I don't want to believe it. He wouldn't be friends with these vulgar people. He wouldn't have this voice, these gestures, these facial expressions. Nor that form, nor that color. He wouldn't bother being so banal. This superficiality is not at all what I would expect from me, or from him. The all-purpose sentence: "You've met me before," he said it. I say any old thing in reply, thinking with all my might: "Do you often have success with that?"

All the same. As soon as he has left, I busy myself correcting the feeble image I had made for myself before I met him. I hadn't given a damn about what he was really like.

At the next encounter, no longer the slightest effort to adapt. I would almost surprise myself by concluding: He is exactly as I had imagined.

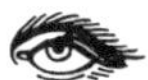

Cutting one's losses

As soon as I get to know them, each one a ferocious beast, they speak out against my most precious treasure. Against the unique unnamable. Against my indefinable reason for being. Nonetheless, I allow them the advantage. But their thirst for prey cannot be appeased; their hunger for my flesh is insatiable. They don't do this with the least nastiness. It's just too strong for me.

I feel them come at speed. A gesture, a word, a nothing — mostly indirect — reveals me to them. They gorge themselves on my tears. They don't leave me even with the wherewithal to suffer. I only have the heart to weep when I have fled from them.

Dear Strangers, keep your distance: I have only you in the world.
"And me? What about me?..." someone shouts: myself.
My beautiful future, the unhoped for reserve, comes to me. Present already past, you who evade me, one moment more respite...
Provided that it's not too late.

CLAUDE CAHUN

AVEUX NON AVENUS

1	Mac Orlan was a friend and admirer of Cahun's uncle, the symbolist writer Marcel Schwob, whose most famous work was, arguably, *Vies imaginaires* [imaginary lives].

2	Isabelle Eberhardt (1877–1904) was a Swiss writer and explorer who traveled extensively in North Africa dressed in male garb, adopting a series of male *noms de plume*. She drowned at the age of just twenty-seven in a flash flood in Aïn-Séfra, a town in the Sahara desert.

3	Wordplay—Cahun uses *mettre en plein dans le vide*, reminiscent of the expression *mettre en plein dans le mille*. *Mille* [a thousand] is the value of the center of the target, the bull's eye.

4	A reference to Cahun's Jewish roots: her father was Jewish but her mother was Catholic. The young Claude (née Lucy Renée Mathilde Schwob) was mostly brought up by her paternal grandmother, Mathilde Cahun, who was Jewish and whose name she took.

5	Claude Cahun had a devoted, lifelong relationship with Marcel Moore (née Suzanne Malherbe). Nonetheless, commentators have tended to interpret this part of the text as evidence of a heterosexual passion for Bob, a Jersey farmworker and fisherman. Scholar Hannah Freed-Thall suggests the references to Bob are playful and tongue-in-cheek and should be read in the context of a virtuosic performance of an unreliable first-person narrator. Amelia Groom aptly observes that Bob could be seen as an object of transmasculine identification: he appears twice in the photomontage for chapter one (at the top, to the right of the detail from a statue, and again in the top right-hand corner), chief among the models of masculinity radiating out from the child image of Cahun.

6	Using the informal second person, *tu*, Cahun is addressing her lifelong companion, Marcel Moore.

7	A pun. Cahun uses the phrase *sortir... de ses gonds*, which has the additional colloquial meaning of "to get into a fury."

8	Icarus, in Greek mythology, fell to his death when he flew too close to the sun, melting the wax that held his artificial wings together.

9	Saccard is a fictional character created by Émile Zola in *Les Rougon-Macquart*, his cycle of twenty novels.

10	Pyrrhus, a legendary figure described by Plutarch, was said to have one continuous bone where his upper teeth should have been.

11	Flavius Arcadius (377–408 CE) was Emperor of the eastern part of the Roman Empire from 395 CE until his death.

12	"Complicity," in this context, refers to a kind of partnership between the speaker and the historical figures mentioned in the two previous notes.

13	Giant King of Thrace, renowned in Greek mythology for his for magnificent, wild, uncontrollable and, most significantly, man-eating mares.

14	"Woe to the conquered," from the Latin phrase *vae victis*.

15	Cahun often associates herself with Salome. John the Baptist is invariably the man desired by women, as in Oscar Wilde's version of the Biblical tale in his play *Salome*.

16	*Arrivez les troisième classes*: using the verb *arriver* turns this into a pun on the class system—an *arriviste* is a "social climber."

17	A possible reference to "he ploughed her and she cropped," (Agrippa's crude description of Anthony's liaison with Cleopatra) in Shakespeare's *Anthony and Cleopatra*, Act 2, Scene 2, Line 228).

18   Wordplay—*herbes folles* means "rank weeds" but *folle* is also the feminine form of *fou*, meaning "mad."

19   A pun on an expression *à bouche que veux-tu*, which denotes kissing with great abandon.

20   The arrow refers to Cupid's arrow of love; it is also a common symbol for Apollo—his being, among other things, the god of poetry.

21   Wordplay—*aimant*, means "loving" and, as a noun, "magnet."

22   Wordplay on *camarde*, meaning "pug-nosed" and, as a noun (informal/slang) "death."

23   A reference to her own and her father's profiles. Cahun chose to identify with her father, who was Jewish, rather than her mother, a Catholic.

24   This passage had already been published as *Carnaval en chambre* [carnival in the bedroom] in a review called *La Ligne du coeur* (Nantes, 1926). The family was very involved with the Nantes carnival; Cahun's father was part of the organizing committee. The annual event may have informed her abiding interest in masks and disguise.

25   The reference is to the seven circles of hell in Dante's *Divine Comedy*.

26   The theme of insanity is important in Cahun's writing. Her mother, Victorine Courbebaisse (known as 'Toinette), was institutionalized when Cahun was just eight years old.

27   A small port in Brittany where, like many people from Nantes, the Schwob family used to spend their holidays. Described at length in *Vues et Visions* [views and visions].

28   Cahun was thirty-three at the time of writing. She is conflating herself with the murdered child, possibly alluding to the physically and emotionally abusive treatment she received from her mother during her childhood.

29   The name given by the Spartans to their degraded and abused serfs. The connotation in this context is possibly that the Spartans made the Hilotes drunk in order to dissuade their own children from drinking alcohol after having witnessed the Hilotes' drunken antics.

30   A reference to "*Impression fausse*" [false impression], a poem by Paul Verlaine.

31   Wordplay—a less usual meaning of *psyche* is "swing mirror."

32   Fragments put together to make a whole, like a mosaic, is a motif that recurs throughout *Cancelled Confessions*.

33   Allusion to the scandalous novel *Le Jardin des supplices* [torture garden], 1899, by Octave Mirbeau, a friend of Cahun. The whole passage reflects the aesthetic decadence that characterized this school of writing. Cahun often alludes to the pleasure of pain, leading some to suggest an appetite for BDSM.

34   Parsifal, or Percival, is one of King Arthur's legendary Knights of the Round Table, most famous for his participation in the quest for the Holy Grail.

35   Gordian Tangle, or Gordian Knot, is a legend associated with Alexander the Great. It is often used as a metaphor for an intractable problem, solved by a bold stroke.

36   Allusion to the celebrated *les deux infinis* passage in Pascal's *Pensées* [thoughts] which investigates the duality of the infinite—the vastness of outer space and the smallness of our human inner space.

37   Narcissus, in Greek mythology, renowned for his beauty, was said to have worshipped his own reflection; his story was introduced into English Victorian homoerotic culture by Oscar Wilde, Havelock Ellis, and others.

38   Tantalus killed his own son and served his flesh to the Gods in a stew. As a punishment, Zeus condemned him to be eternally hungry and thirsty in Hades, immobilized on his feet in a pool of water, with a fruit tree just out of reach. This myth is the origin of the word "tantalizing."

39   *Pris dans les glaces* is a wordplay on the double meaning of glaces—"mirrors" and "ice

fields." When speaking of a boat, *pris dans les glaces* means "icebound."

40   A mixture of allusions to two Greek myths concerning Penelope and Arachne.

41   Cahun uses the word *pédéraste* which, in her time, would have had the classical connotation of the love of an older man for a younger man. Today, there is a suggestion of pedophilia which is unlikely to have been intended by Cahun, hence the selection of the word "homosexual" instead.

42   A Greek writer much admired by Cahun's uncle, Marcel Schwob.

43   Praxiteles was a classical sculptor; he made his Venus around 360 BCE.

44   A typical Cahunian play on words, *espèces fausses—espèces* means "species" and "variety," but can also mean the bread and wine used in Holy Communion; fausse means "false" or "fake."

45   Cahun seems to be referring to Victor Hugo's poem "*Le Feu du ciel*" [fire from heaven] which is prefaced by a quote from Genesis: "And the Lord caused a rain of sulfur and fire to fall upon Sodom and Gomorrah."

46   *Semence philosophale*, a play on *pierre philosophale*—the philosopher's stone that alchemists longed to find. *Semence* means "seed" and "semen" (in a medical context).

47   The Auriga, from which Cahun has derived this name, is a famous statue of a male Greek charioteer (also known as the Charioteer of Delphi). In the top right-hand corner of the photomontage for this section, we find the arm of this statue, holding reins.

48   Sakyamuni, more commonly known as the Buddha. Cahun and Moore were friends with Grace Constant Lounsbery, who founded a Buddhism society in France.

49   Jersey—Cahun and Moore frequently vacationed on the Channel Island before permanently relocating there in 1937.

50   A well-known quote by Philippe Néricault Destouches, 1680–1754: *La critique est aisée, et l'Art est difficile* [criticism is easy, and art is difficult].

51   Cahun emphasizes and contrasts the gender of the two nouns, *l'âme* (the "soul," feminine) and *le corps* (the "body," masculine), hence the decision to translate as "he" rather than "it" in this instance.

52   A reference to La Fontaine's "The Hare and the Tortoise" when the tortoise comments that the hare has "run in vain."

53   A reference to the "derangement of the senses," proposed by Arthur Rimbaud.

54   This is part of the first line of the fifth verse of Charles Baudelaire's poem "Moesta et errabunda": *mais le vert paradis des amours enfantines* [but the green paradise of childhood loves].

55   Cahun uses the word *peine*, which also means "punishment."

56   This is a more cynical retelling of the encounter Baudelaire describes in "Le joujou du pauvre" [the poor boy's plaything] in *Le Spleen de Paris* [Paris spleen].

57   The Ferryman's dog is the three-headed Cerberus who guarded the entrance to hell on the other side of the River Styx. When Psyche descended to the underworld, she was advised to carry honey cakes to placate him.

58   Prospective priests of the earth goddess Cybele castrated themselves using special ornamented clamps. Post-castration, they adorned themselves with feminine attire: jewelry, colorful robes, and turbans or tiaras over hairstyles common among the women of their day.

59   A reference to Immanuel Kant's concept of the categorical imperative as the determinant for the actions of human beings.

60   *Lacs*, as well as meaning "lakes," can also mean a kind of trap.

61 *Ataraxia*—a Greek word meaning the absence of confusion or disturbance.

62 As in *alma mater*, meaning "gentle," "nurturing."

63 Previously published in the February 1926 edition of *Le Mercure de France*.

64 Cahun has reversed the old saying *lâcher la proie pour l'ombre* [let go the prey for a shadow], meaning to give up a real advantage for an illusory promise.

65 A pun—*faire peau neuve* also means to "turn over a new leaf."

66 Cahun refuses the conventional use of a capital H when "He" refers to God.

67 Cahun admired the life and works of Oscar Wilde, whose literary influence is evident in this dramatized section.

68 R.P. —*révérend père* [reverend father].

69 *Ne pas manger de ce pain-là* [don't eat any of that bread] is a saying denoting a refusal to do something because it is wrong and tends to corrupt. The pun—on the host in Holy Communion—is obvious and irreverent.

70 Cahun may be imagining an old-fashioned character describing "new-fangled" X-rays.

71 Reference to the proverb *on n'est jamais si bien servi que par soi-même* [no one treats one as well as one treats oneself].

72 *S'ouvre à deux battants*: this improbable image comes from the phrase *ouvrir les portes à deux battants* [to fling the gates/doors wide open]—a figurative expression meaning opening oneself to all opportunities and possibilities.

73 Wordplay on "presumption of innocence."

74 Wordplay on "to be in a state of legitimate defense."

75 Wordplay—*syncope* also means "fainting fit."

76 An authentic French proverb.

77 This is particularly fine example of Cahun's characteristic wordplay. *Les abeilles ont des fleurets mouchetés: les abeilles* [bees] have *fleurets*—meaning swords but also sounding like *fleurs* [flowers]; *mouchetés* means swords with a kind of protective stopper over the point, but also sounds like *mouche* [fly]. Furthermore, all these words rhyme: *abeilles, fleurets, mouchetés.*

78 Wordplay on *trompe la mort* [cheat death].

79 The following passage had been published earlier in a sequence of writings entitled *Éphémérides* in *Le Mercure de France*, January 1927. (François Leperlier, editor, *Claude Cahun, Écrits.* Jean-Michel Place, Paris, 2002, p.465).

80 A biblical reference to the parable of the workers in the vineyard (Matthew 20)—those who arrived at the eleventh hour were paid the same as those who had toiled since dawn.

81 As in English, "sublimate" has two main meanings: the chemical process by which solids are transformed into gas without passing through a liquid stage and the psychological process whereby a primitive impulse (such as a sexual urge) is unconsciously transformed into something higher or more socially acceptable, as per Freud.

82 A well-known French saying—*la plus belle fille du monde ne peut offrir que ce qu'elle a* [even the most beautiful girl in the world can only offer what she has], i.e. her body.

83 The phrase she uses is a *double détente* [a gun that is fired twice in quick succession], itself a pun on "double entendre."

84 Referencing the legend in which Alexander the Great went to visit Diogenes—an ascetic who lived in a burial urn—and asked him if there was anything he could do for him, Diogenes replied: "You could move away out of the sun so as not to cast a shadow over me."

85 Wingless birds of the Kiwi genus. Victory is traditionally shown with wings.

86 Madame Putiphar, central character in Pétrus Borel's eponymous 1838 novel, who throws a handsome young Irishman into a dungeon for life when he rejects her lascivious advances.

87 Daphnis and Chloe, according to Greek mythology, did not know how to have sex.

88 Biographical note: Cahun's mother eventually converted from Catholicism to Protestantism.

89 The Latin word *cinedus* (plural *cinaedi*) referred to an effeminate, erotic, subversive male performer. The cinedi were associated with gender and sexual deviance by Roman moralists. The word is closely related to the Greek *kinaidos*, which describes a man considered unmanly or sexually passive.

90 Sappho, female archaic Greek lyric poet (probably 630–570 BCE), born on the island of Lesbos.

91 Cahun often turns biblical phrases upside down; in this case—"knock and it shall be opened unto you."

92 When Cahun submitted the original manuscript of *Aveux non Avenus* to Jean Paulhan, at the Parisian publishing house Gallimard, he rejected it, complaining it was of *un genre indéterminé* [an indeterminate genre] and would therefore be difficult to classify and market. What follows is Cahun's response!

93 A reference to a variation on Aesop's fable "The Wolf in Sheep's Clothing" wherein the wolf covers himself in flour to disguise himself as a sheep. *Montrer patte blanche* [to show a white paw] has become an expression in French denoting someone who covers their malevolent true intentions with an appearance of innocence.

94 Humor derived from the fact that normally these phrases would refer to cats rather than angels.

95 Wordplay on the common saying *autres temps, autres moeurs* [other times, other morals].

96 Apart from the obvious sexual connotations, this passage also refers to Cahun's anorexia, where food would have been viewed as a perversion, forced on her by adults.

97 A reference to the duel with Valentin in Charles Gounod's opera, *Faust*. Mephistopheles tells Faust, "Only strike him, Doctor. I will make sure to parry."

98 The revolving table is a means of divination, communicating with the spirits of the dead.

99 This is a quote from *Comme il fait beau!* [what lovely weather], a Dada play by André Breton, Robert Desnos and Benjamin Péret. Cahun frequented Dada events and performances in Paris in the early 1920s.

100 A children's game in which the participants must determine if a chosen object can fly or not, a game which appealed to the imaginations of the Dadaists (a long section involving improbable flying objects appears in *Comme il fait beau!*).

101 A historical allusion. In the previous sentence Cahun uses the word *Allemand* (translated as "German"); here she uses *germain* which was in use until the late Middle Ages when the borders of *la Germanie* changed. In addition, there is a play on words—*cousin germain* also means "first cousin."

102 A pun—*ongle droit* [right nail] sounds like *angle droit* [right angle]. They are leaning on their right nails as they hold their pens, like children in the classroom—a comical image that pervades this whole passage.

103 This is one of several allusions to surrealist games—in this case, the exquisite corpse, devised in 1925 by Breton and others.

104 A children's song set on an imaginary boat lost at sea: lots are drawn to decide whom the others should eat first. Like the rest of the passage, there are also political allusions to the contemporary situation in Europe with which Cahun was fully conversant.

105 The suggestion is that she has castrated her father; the same implication is present in the description of cutting off curlews' beaks since she inherited her father's fine, curved nose.

106 From Molière's *Le Bourgeois gentilhomme* [the bourgeois gentleman], in which the central character, middle-class M. Jourdain, attempts

to emulate the mannerisms and speech of the aristocracy with comedic results.

107   A pun on "ivory tower."

108   The following passage is not a call to war; it is an anti-war statement.

109   Cahun may be referring to her collaborations with Marcel Moore, cocreator of the photomontages in this book and other works. Until relatively recently, these works were attributed solely to Cahun.

110   Opotherapy—a medical practice at the time, consisted of administering desiccated healthy animal tissues or juices, or the active principles extracted from them, via the gastrointestinal route or by injection.

111   The word Cahun uses here—*glace* —can mean both "ice" and "mirror." Both have resonances with the rest of the passage.

112   The Hebrew name of John the Baptist, and the name given to him in Oscar Wilde's *Salome*.

113   *Plus de peur que de mal*—a succinct phrase used when somebody escapes unharmed from danger, meaning something like "it could have been terrible, but in the end we were afraid for no reason."

114   A reference to the book *Les hors nature; moeurs contemporaines* [the unnatural ones; contemporary morals] by the novelist Rachilde, with whom Cahun was acquainted through her father and uncle, Maurice and Marcel Schwob.

115   Pontius Pilate was the governor of the Roman Judea province 26–36 CE. In modern times, he is best known as the man who presided over the trial of Jesus and ordered his crucifixion.

116   An old fairground game where the aim was to "kill" all the figures.

117   *Reductio ad absurdum* [reduction to the absurd]—a method of philosophical reasoning often used by Aristotle, also known as an apagogic argument.

118   A "second" was the trusted person chosen by each combatant in a duel. The second made all of the arrangements then accompanied his combatant to the duel in order to make sure the fight was fair and correctly run.

119   This is a satirical reference to the formal closings the French adhere to when writing letters.

120   Possibly Sodom and Gomorrah.

121   A pun—*incarné* means "incarnate" but also "ingrown."

122   The choke-pear was an iron torture instrument used in the Spanish Inquisition. Shaped like a pear, it was inserted into the victim's mouth, anus or vagina (especially for women accused of being witches) where it was expanded by turning a key. Some also had spikes which emerged as the key was turned, ensuring it could not be removed.

123   Wordplay—*la mort* [death] and *l'amour* [love] sound exactly the same when spoken.

124   Avoiding binary gender in French is much more difficult than in English. In *Cancelled Confessions*, Cahun improvises a neutral positionality, most notably by alternating between masculine and feminine endings that signal the gender of the subject: at one moment, the feminine—*je me suis mise au lit* [I went to bed]; and at another the masculine—*je deviens fou* [I become mad]. It's a strategy applied to not only the first person but also the third person subject, for example when describing the angel (pp.54, 124, 139, 170). Cahun also exploits occasions when gender in French designates the object and not the subject. For instance, in the sex scene in chapter one, the gender of the lover is left intentionally ambiguous: "an arm [*son bras*], all trembling, explored my heart" (p.14). Scholars are increasingly interested in Cahun as a key figure in the trans/nonbinary avant-garde. See, for instance, Amelia Groom's introduction to this volume, Juno Richards's essay, "Claude Cahun's Pronouns," in *Modernism/modernity*

Print Plus, 6.1 (April 2021) and Hannah Freed-Thall's forthcoming essay on *Aveux non Avenus* to be published in a catalog accompanying the Museum of Modern Art's 2026 exhibition of modernist artists' books.

125 A pun on *eau de vie*, a kind of alcoholic spirit.

126 Wordplay on *confirme* [proves]; *l'infirme* [weakens it].

127 The literal meaning is "for the house/home," a phrase used when one represents oneself, for example, in court.

128 "Ariane" is the name given to Bluebeard's wife in *Ariane et Barbe-Bleue*, a 1907 opera by Paul Dukas, based on a symbolist play by Maurice Maeterlinck. In a 1929 production of a play by Pierre Albert Birot, Cahun played Bluebeard's wife (named "Elle" rather than "Ariane" here). Photographic documentation of Cahun in this role is featured in the photomontage for chapter one of this book. In the original legend, Bluebeard has seven wives, six of whom he murdered.

129 According to Pliny the Elder's 77 CE *The Natural History*, Chapter 14 (12): As it was unlawful for women to drink alcohol in ancient Rome, Egnatius Mecenius killed his wife for drinking wine and suffered nothing for the deed.

130 Biblical reference to separating the wheat from the chaff.

131 "Holocaust" did not have the immense historical significance it has now. It meant a sacrifice by fire in which the victim is totally consumed.

132 *Über Alles* [above all else] is commonly associated with the first line of the German national anthem: *Deutschland, Deutschland über alles*.

133 *Charlot*—affectionate nickname for Charlie Chaplin, also a "clown."

134 An *oubliette* was found in most medieval castles: an underground prison where people were literally forgotten and left to die.

135 A hecatomb was an ancient Greek ritualistic slaughter of 100 cattle.

136 Reference to the children's game "catch me if you can."

137 The medical term for swallowing.

138 An example of Cahun's prescient concerns about human impact on the environment.

139 *Ab ovo* [from the egg], meaning to start (e.g. a chronology) at the earliest possible point.

140 Plutarch (46–120 CE) was a Greek historian and writer, best known for his book *The Lives of Famous Men*.

141 "To work for the King of Prussia" is a French idiom meaning to work for nothing, for peanuts.

142 In Greek mythology, Marsyas was a satyr who challenged Apollo to a contest of music to be judged by the muses. They agreed the winner could treat the defeated party in any way he chose. Marsyas lost and was flayed alive in a cave. His blood turned into the river Marsyas in ancient Phrygia, part of modern Turkey.

143 Wordplay—*écorché* [flayed] can also mean an artist's anatomical model.

144 A reference to the Latin saying *panem et circenses* [bread and spectacle], which was all the Roman élite considered necessary to satisfy the people.

145 Children's game in which the small bones from a sheep are tossed up and caught on the back of the hand.

146 Cahun is imagining a date with death.

147 Wordplay—the tortoise also refers to the Roman testudo (or tortoise) formation where shields formed a protective wall to cover a battalion of soldiers.

148 Marguerite, seduced by Faust; Titine, the heroine of a popular song.

149 Eurydice, in Greek mythology, was the wife of Orpheus.

150 Orpheus was believed to be one of the chief poets and musicians of antiquity as well as the inventor of the lyre.

151 Beatrice Portinari, the guide through Paradise in Dante's *Divine Comedy*.

152 Reference to a popular saying—*courir deux lièvres à la fois* [chasing two hares at the same time], meaning trying to do two things at once.

153 "Casting out the nines" is an archaic mathematical method for checking additions.

154 Echo, in Greek mythology, was a mountain nymph who loved her own voice.

155 In Norse mythology, the Valkyrie were a group of female warriors and harbingers of war. They served the god Odin who sent them to battlefields to select those worthy of a place in Valhalla (the afterworld) from among the slain.

156 A pun on the word *préservatif* which can also mean "condom."

157 Erich von Stroheim (1885–1957)—film actor, later director. Well-known for his villainous roles, he starred in *The Devil's Passkey* in 1920, and *Souls for Sale* in 1923, both titles having resonance with this poem-essay.

158 The word she uses is *la roue* which usually means "wheel," but can also mean, as in this case, the circular display of a peacock's tail feathers.

159 An oblique reference to the forced-labor camp on Devil's Island in the French colony of Guyana, whose capital is Cayenne.

160 A "milk brother" is someone unrelated who suckles the same woman's milk.

161 Two-faced Janus was the Roman god of transitions and dualities, facing both the future and the past. Usually depicted with a key, symbolizing his protection of doors, gates, etc.

162 A reference to Max Stirner's thesis that while humanity killed God, the essence of God is replaced with the essence of humanity. Stirner (1806–1856) was a post-Hegelian philosopher and is considered one of the forerunners of anarchism.

163 A pun on trompe l'oeil—*l'âme* meaning "soul."

Translator's Note
SUSAN DE MUTH

It has often been said that translation is the deepest form of reading. Of all the texts I have worked with, *Aveux non Avenus* is the one that most rewards such close study. Edited and reedited by the author over a ten-year period, the text is a web of tightly woven, self-contained short pieces of writing that elude categorization.[1]

Making a translation of such work is particularly challenging. As a writer, Cahun combines concentrated economy with great originality, and her sentences, as well as her ideas, often demand a great deal of application if their meaning and value are to be fully understood and appreciated. Having unwrapped Cahun's thoughts and observations from their complex packaging of words and images, the translator is then bound to rewrap them in a similar fashion but in another language altogether. This process is all the more challenging given Cahun's liberal use of colloquialisms, aphorisms, puns and wordplay. Where these are impossible to translate I have provided explanatory endnotes.

In art as in life, Cahun rejected all forms of constraint, including those imposed by "truth"... and grammar! Her "confessions" are often briskly retracted at the last moment: long passages of angst are undercut by a facetious postscript which is itself unreliable. Her grammatical adventures are equally challenging: there are abrupt, inexplicable changes in tense, for example, and she frequently slides from the confessional first person ("I") to the third person ("she" or "he").

The frequent shifts in gender are not always translatable into English (for example, when it is indicated only by the masculine or feminine form of an adjective). The sometimes playful, sometimes serious insistence on gender complexity and fluidity make Cahun an important figure for contemporary social movements and discourses on queer and trans identities and histories.

Cahun's writing style also presents dilemmas for the translator. There is a conscious awkwardness in certain passages—a deliberate undermining of our linguistic expectations, whether through subversion of grammar, logic, gender, value or simply the everyday associations of words and phrases. Cahun uses this device frequently; it jolts you, makes you go beyond the usual boundaries of thought and language. Linguistic distortion and prior association are two of the means by which she "addresses the subconscious," as noted by her French biographer, François Leperlier.[2] The translator has to decide whether to retain the awkwardness of these parts of the text or present them in a more "readable" manner in English. I have opted for the former.

I do not want to give the reader the idea that these are turgid, "difficult" writings. On the contrary, Cahun is an adept and often hilarious entertainer (she and her partner Marcel Moore[3] enjoyed several theatrical collaborations with Pierre Albert-Birot). Her style of writing changes abruptly as she delves into her "mental theater"[4] to recount extracts of bizarrely comical conversations, hyperbolic mythologies of her own invention, dark perversions of familiar fairy tales and wittily subversive reworkings of stories from the Bible. I hope I have been able to convey these shifts in voice and tone, as well as the humour that runs through a significant part of the text.

The cultural, as well as historical, context in which a work is written (and read) presents its own challenges for the translator. Cahun sometimes addresses the reader's subconscious, relying on contemporaneous associations of ideas, images and meaning; naturally these change with a relocation from post-WWI France to the twenty-first century English-speaking world. Where appropriate, I have provided notes.

While some "subversive" writing loses its ability to shock as time progresses, Cahun avoids this fate in *Cancelled Confessions* through the sheer originality of her imagination. While the notion of a "gamy host" (p.202) may offend a Catholic more than a non-Catholic, the image remains extremely perturbing and rich in subtextual allusions (to transubstantiation, for example). Likewise, much of Cahun's imagery contains, or leads to, a rich web of associated meaning or thematic references in the manner of a metaphysical conceit, which I have endeavored to reproduce.

Certain characters reappear (often in different guises) throughout the book, but there is no narrative cohesion in what is, essentially, a collection of fragments. A sense of unity is provided, instead, by Cahun's recurrent themes. These themes, such as mirrors, duality, masks, disgust with the physical body (Cahun was probably anorexic), and so on, inform not only the exceptionally visual, often cinematic, writing, but also the photomontages that accompany the text. These were made together with Cahun's partner and artistic collaborator, Marcel Moore. Cahun referred to the photomontages as "visual poems," and it is to be hoped that the intricate relationship between the images and the text in *Cancelled Confessions* will be observed and enjoyed by the reader.

Susan de Muth is a translator specializing in the early twentieth century avant-garde. She runs Thin Man Press and lives in London.

notes

1 Jean Paulhan described the book as being of an "indeterminate genre" when he rejected it for publication by Gallimard… Cahun delightedly reused the phrase as a subheading in *Cancelled Confessions* (p.144).

2 François Leperlier, *Claude Cahun: L'Exotisme intérieure*, Paris, Fayard, 2006, p.173.

3 aka Suzanne Malherbe, Cahun's lifelong lover and artistic collaborator.

4 François Leperlier, *Claude Cahun: L'Exotisme intérieure*, Paris, Fayard, 2006, p.343.

We come out of our splendid isolation, lend ourselves to the world
AMELIA GROOM

A veux non Avenus, translated here as *Cancelled Confessions (or Disavowals)*, was written, compiled and illustrated in Paris in the 1920s and first published in 1930. The author, Claude Cahun, was initially encouraged to write a confessional memoir by the publisher and bookseller Adrienne Monnier.[1] "You have told me to write a confession… I believe that I have understood in what manner, in what form you envision this confession (in sum: without deceit of any sort)," Cahun wrote in a letter to Monnier in 1926. "Don't get your hopes up," they added. Two years later, Cahun presented Monnier with the manuscript and asked if she would consider publishing it and writing a preface. Both requests were denied.[2]

If Monnier did have hopes for an autobiographical confession "without deceit of any sort," it's not hard to imagine why she would have rejected *Cancelled Confessions*. At the very outset of the book, Cahun warns that there will be no sincere and factual first-person account of an authentic subject. Rather than "burden myself with all the paraphernalia of facts"—rather than offering "humble and truthful testaments" that would "surely touch somebody's heart"—they would prefer to "trace the wake of vessels in the air, the pathway over the waters, the pupil's mirage."

This is a book of "false impressions" and seeing "confusedly, partially." A book where "memory swells in vain, gorged with its false treasures." A book where "makeup is a must." In defiance of any pressure Cahun might have felt to write their confessions "without deceit of any sort," this is a book that relishes in the aesthetics of trickery, disguise, hallucination, inconsistency, contradiction, and lies. "I'm such a good liar!" Cahun enthuses in one of the fragments. In another, we meet a prince who complains to his dads—two sorcerer husbands who made their son from slugs and magic—"about an excess of honesty which caused his senses to render everything that came near him, everything he touched, sterile."

Cahun's words of warning to Monnier—"don't get your hopes up"—can be extended to readers today: if you're looking for linear autobiographical narration, if you're looking for "humble and truthful testaments," if you're looking for a memoir that offers a cohesive account of an individual self, you won't find it here. There is a form of selfhood presented in *Cancelled Confessions*, but it's a thoroughly impure, intersubjective, and decentralized selfhood that is always being built up, and undone, through overt artifice, layers of negation, shattered dispersals, provisional reassemblings, ecological expansiveness and messy entanglements.

The book's kaleidoscopic text is pieced together from diverse fragments— some of them drawn from (though not attributed as) materials Cahun had previously published elsewhere. Form is all over the place: There are philosophical and subversive theological musings, aphorisms and fables, letters and dialogues, dreams and hymns, nightmares and jokes. There's a sarcastic job listing (the "vacant position" offers "success, wealth—maybe power" to those who "stick to the well-behaved, necessary boundary marks of a well-brought-up way of thinking")— and there's a derisive recipe for a love potion ("do you think you'll make a good stock of love by boiling up the lovers' chastity belt, their breakup letters, their crocodile tears and purple sage? Add the playthings of your solitary nights, and serve cold"). Desires for categorization are constantly undermined (Cahun writes bemusedly about people for whom "a sticker is obligatory" because "faced with unlabeled products they become completely disoriented"). Closure is always deferred ("Why hasten toward eternal conclusions?" Cahun asks, "Life's role is to leave me uncompleted").

For readers of *Cancelled Confessions* today, a century after its parts were pulled together, the pages are writhing with life and secrets—and calling out for new readings. As a confessions-cancelling exercise in polyvocality, the book is bursting with metamorphoses and propelled by constant shifts in (and proliferations of) perspective. At times inscrutable but often hilarious, it's quick and sassy and queer as fuck. It's also dense with literary and Biblical references, esoterism and classical mythology, modern psychiatry and European political history, and various philosophical digressions and convolutions. Some guidance on how to approach the text might be found in a fragment of chapter five, wherein Cahun describes "a well-behaved child" who dreams about "the inhumane, the monstrous, the impossible," as well as the ordinary ("the most ordinary life has its adventures, its records, its wonders") with "permission to skim, to skip pages, pages and pages—and to read between the lines, at her leisure."

An integral part of this artist book is the series of photogravure collage images that were made in dialogue with the text—one for each of the nine chapters, plus one frontispiece. These were composed by the illustrator Marcel Moore, who was Cahun's partner and artistic collaborator.[3] Like Cahun's collaged text, the images are gathered from multiple sources and constituted through fracture and fragmentation. There are newspaper and magazine clippings, X-ray images, playing cards, bits of found text, a scientific graph and hand-drawn illustrations alongside cut-out photos of cats and prickly pears and dismembered classical sculptures. Body parts—hands, mouths, eyes, feet, heads, legs—are isolated as shapes that circulate on their own and come together into new composite entities. Lips form petals around an anus; eleven heads extend from a single neck, stacked up in a phallic protrusion. New images are found through inversions, rotations, and duplications. Scale is all messed up. Shadows and reflections abound.

And then there are the photographs of Cahun, which the couple made together.[4] Cahun in an array of many-gendered guises and expressions pursued through theatrical makeup, props, costumes, and masks. Some of these images come from the couple's involvement with the Théâtre Ésotérique company in Paris—and with Le Plateau, Pierre Albert-Birot's avant-garde theater ensemble, where Cahun's acting roles included "Elle" [wife], "Le Monsieur" [the man], and "Le Diable" [the devil].[5] Photomontage offered a space for the artists to continue the proliferations and bodily reconfigurations they initiated in the costumed portraits. Cut into pieces and brought into new sets of relations, the body is understood as a material that can be taken apart, stretched out, and reshaped so that it extends beyond the familiar human form, and beyond the lonely confines of the neatly delineated individual self.

Part of the problem with the normative construction of selfhood, this book suggests, is that it can be an obstacle to the abundance found in relationality. "I no longer exist?" Cahun writes, "Perfect! Now nothing can come between us." While *Cancelled Confessions* frequently returns to the site of the self (and the myth of the self-loving Narcissus), the interest is never in the self as something that can be separated from its ecologies of desire and dependency. When Cahun writes in the final chapter about trying to see their body from an external perspective, they immediately qualify that they mean "my body with its dependencies." In seeking divestment from the authoritative sovereignty of autonomous selfhood, Cahun and Moore find enjoyment in a mode of selfhood that is accompanied and permeable; a selfhood that can be reinvented and extended via proxies and prosthetics; a selfhood that is environmentally distributed and playfully reconfigured through splits, inversions, proliferations, and scatterings.

The original title, *Aveux non Avenus*, is essentially untranslatable. This is the case with much of Cahun's writing, which is often thick with wordplay and multiple meanings. While the 2007 publication of de Muth's translation had *Disavowals* as the primary English title, here it's *Cancelled Confessions*. There was some deliberation about this change. Wouldn't it be confusing to introduce a different name at this stage, when *Disavowals* has been taken up as the title in the anglophone literature for some time (for instance, with Jennifer Shaw's 2013 book *Reading Claude Cahun's Disavowals*)? My position on the matter is that there's something appropriately Cahunian in allowing for change and multiple names (they write explicitly, in chapter two, about the desire to "try out all my names").

I also think *Cancelled Confessions* is a better translation. It refers to the confessional literary genre and the vital aspect of its negation—and (unlike *Disavowals*) it maintains the important aspect of alliteration: from *Aveux non Avenus* (AA) to *Cancelled Confessions* (CC). As their chosen masculine and gender neutral names attest, Claude Cahun (CC) and Marcel Moore (MM) had a special affinity for alliteration. This affinity can be traced back to their earliest work; the first artist book they made together—a study of seaside apparitions and time-travelling hallucinations, with text by Cahun and images by Moore—was titled *Vues et Visions* or *Views and Visions* (VV). Structured as a series of pairs or doublings of poems that mirror and diverge from each other, the text for *Vues et Visions* was first published in a literary journal in 1914, when Cahun was a nineteen-year-old going by an earlier alliterative chosen name, Claude Courlis (CC).

The fixation on the alliterative form is part of the broader dynamics of doubling, multiplying, pairing, and mirroring that play out in Cahun and Moore's approach to language, as well as in their image-making. In a double-headed portrait that features (doubly) in the photomontage for chapter three, for instance, Cahun appears–looking very post-gender with their hair and eyebrows shaved off–from two different angles at once. This is a self at odds with itself; a freakishly alliterative self that comes out from itself through simultaneous duplication and divergence.[6]

Alliteration enacts difference birthed from ostensible sameness, with the repetition of the same letter leading into a whole new word. This is also how mirroring works throughout Cahun and Moore's oeuvre; the doubling of the image presents an opportunity for its redirection and alteration. Many mirrors and mirror images can be found in the pages of *Cancelled Confessions*, but none of them offer coherent or reliable replications. Rather, mirroring functions as a device for the distortion, fragmentation, and proliferating displacement of the (self-)image—as when Cahun's text takes us to "the impossible realized in a magic mirror"; to a mirror that "refuses me the comfort of my reflection"; to a "distorting mirror"; and to a narrow mirror that shows "a part of it only."

Water surfaces, similarly, are returned to as sites that can reflect the light while also producing dynamic effects of fragmentary ripples, blurred boundaries, and occluded visions. This is a theme in Cahun and Moore's very watery *Views and Visions*, and it runs through *Cancelled Confessions* as well.[7] At one point in the text, Cahun describes an oceanic horizon "lost in the waves' mist." Elsewhere, they enthuse about the optical fragmentation that the sea can bring about: "A man in the sea! A bit of flesh floats, an arm already shattered by refraction." The emphasis on reflections and refractions has to do with the destabilization of the image and the possibility of scattering the self–as Cahun put it in this brief passage (which moves, characteristically, through twists and turns and unapologetic lying):

> *Individualism? Narcissism? Certainly. My best characteristic, the one and only intentional fidelity I am capable of. You don't care? I'm lying anyway: I scatter myself too widely for that.*

MYSELF (for want of anything better) is the title of the book's second chapter. In the first of a pair of subsequent sections of this chapter that are both titled "Self-Love" (right before a section that is titled "Narcissus and Narcissus"), Cahun writes that the death of Narcissus, in the classical myth, "has always seemed totally incomprehensible to me." Narcissus's problem, Cahun proposes, was not that he had too much self-love; it was that he never found the self-love that is "fulfilled in an egoism for two, for many, for all, in the universal orgy." This is a radical reframing of the idea of self-love, moving the self out of myopic isolation and opening it up to the other—and to a cosmic orgy. If the beautiful Narcissus had been able to sense himself as ecologically enmeshed and extended, Cahun suggests, he wouldn't have had to die withered and alone:

Oh Narcissus, you could love yourself in everything: sun, your brother, even more beautiful in the weary night, who reflects a pallor on the moon which he never wearies of admiring; moon, who can only see his body in the lake where he lies stretched out until dawn; all colors scattered and each seeks out the most faithful copy of itself among the valley's multicolored columbines; honeys that the bees, your sisters, are so partial to, and where the flowers seek out their fragrance.

This is a landscape of mirroring and mimicry—of borrowed images, of refracted and redirected light, of playful affinities and affections—through which Cahun offers an alternative to the deadlock of a man looking only at his own mirror image, as it looks only back at him. Rather than be confined within this isolated loop, Cahun suggests to Narcissus, you could love yourself in the sun who admires the moon who mirrors the light of the sun but also redirects it onto the surface of the lake, until daybreak makes the colors scatter through the valley; colors that look for themselves in the flowers which mirror the scent of the honey in order to please the honey-making bees (whose bodies disperse the pollen of the flowers, and so on).

It's as if Narcissus is invited to learn from the scattered ways of Echo, and avoid an unnecessary ("incomprehensible") death by coming into responsive relation with and through the landscape. "We come out of our splendid isolation, lend ourselves to the world," Cahun declares (in a section of chapter six subtitled "Singular Plural"). Through their (mis)reading of the classical myth of Narcissus, they present an expanded field of ever-shifting, nonlinear relations; a field of relations that brings the subject out of themselves, and into an ecologically entangled setting that can undermine the systems of identity that normally seek to isolate and categorize the modern subject (including, for instance, the binary gender system; imagine trying to assign an immutable gender to the moonlight rippling on the lake as it relates to the varied colors and fragrances of the flowers appearing at dawn).[8]

Part of Cahun and Moore's dissatisfaction with individualized and idealized figurations of the autonomous self—and part of what was at play in Cahun's refusal (or inability?) to write the confessional memoir that Monnier had encouraged—was their deep suspicion around ideologies of purity. Throughout this book, contamination is a generative force. I already mentioned the slug-born prince from one of Cahun's fairy tales, who complains of an "excess of honesty," which causes everything he touches to become "sterile." Elsewhere in *Cancelled Confessions*, Cahun announces, with frustration and defiance, that "the air without dust and the flowers without odor and the Prince's mouth full of absolute purities suffice and will long suffice to suffocate us."

Ethically and aesthetically, these artists were invested in mess, incompleteness, remnants, ruination, hybridity and filth. "I'm obsessed with the exception," Cahun writes, "I see it as bigger than nature. It's all I see. The rule interests me only for its leftovers with which I make my swill." There is a queer utopian longing in Cahun's embrace of leftovers for their swill (kitchen refuse and food scraps mixed with water for feeding to pigs). They want a world built from the ruins of the present one, for all those who have been left behind:

I was hoping that God would fashion a childlike world especially for the rest of us out of the leftovers of the universe [...] to be used by weaklings, innocents, soldiers discharged for spiritual deficiency, a world where [...] longitudes and latitudes would no longer atrociously bruise the globe [...] I was hoping... But God would not give way on this.

Against any notion of a unified and universalist progress narrative, Cahun longs for a world built from the leftovers, for the outcasts. God, unfortunately, insists on making use of all the "animal, vegetable and mineral by-products, from his overproduction, from his factory of the absolute, from every unknowable thing." But Cahun imagines a world "for the rest of us"; a world that isn't "atrociously bruised" by regimes of homogenizing legibility; a world where the unknowables can remain unknowable and the leftovers can really be left behind and left alone, without being reinstrumentalized in accordance with the existing paradigms.

At one point in *Cancelled Confessions*, Cahun expresses concern that, in using discarded debris to try to piece together new bodies and new worlds, they could end up accidentally reproducing the assumptions of the reality that already exists.

"I've puffed myself up, stretched, padded myself out, made use of my rubbish, all my nail clippings to no avail," they write. "Can I create nothing more than the world in miniature?" Despite these frustrations, though, Cahun remains committed to the capacious, nonnormative, and transformative possibilities of monstrous impurity and forgotten by-products. The "perfect playground for a poet," they write, is "a pond after a storm." The site of poetry, and of play, is a site of muck, collected debris, aftermath, runoff, grime, and mixing. This is not the clear, transparent water of the pond that reflected the face of Narcissus back to him as a stable, isolated and isolating image; rather, it's a murky pond where the broken, leftover pieces of things can form unexpected new relations, and where no one will end up suffocated by "absolute purities."

Amelia Groom is a writer and art historian currently working on a monograph that looks at Cahun and Moore's art and anti-fascist activism through the lenses of queer and trans ecologies. They teach at the University of California, Santa Cruz.

notes

1   Monnier was the founder of La Maison des Amis des Livres, a lending library, bookstore and publishing house that was a hub of the modernist literary scene in Paris during the interwar years. She was also the partner of publisher Sylvia Beach, who founded the Shakespeare and Company bookstore—another literary hub, where Cahun volunteered for a time.

2   Cited in Tirza True Latimer, *Women Together/Women Apart: Portraits of Lesbian Paris*, New Brunswick, New Jersey, and London: Rutgers University Press, 2005, p.82.

3   These images have often been incorrectly attributed to Cahun as the sole author. This erasure of Moore's contribution is also an erasure of the importance of collaboration and messy, relational entanglements, which are central themes in the book. The original title page stated: *illustré d'héliogravures composées par Moore d'après les projets de l'auteur* [illustrated with photogravures composed by Moore based on plans by the author]. The frontispiece image is clearly signed with Moore's name; the others are unsigned.

4   Art historian Tirza True Latimer has demonstrated the extent to which Cahun and Moore worked collaboratively on their photographs. While some institutions and publications have begun to acknowledge Moore as a coauthor, many continue to misidentify the photographs as "self-portraits" with sole authorship. Tirza True Latimer, "Entre Nous: Between Claude Cahun and Marcel Moore," *GLQ: A Journal of Lesbian and Gay Studies* (12:2, 2006), pp.197–216.

5   For an analysis of the significance of the theater in Cahun and Moore's oeuvre see Miranda Welby-Everard, "Imaging the Actor: The Theatre of Claude Cahun," *Oxford Art Journal* (29:1, 2006), pp.1–24.

6   An illustration rendered from this double-headed Cahun portrait also appeared as the cover image for the 1929 Carrefour publication of Dada artist Georges Ribemont-Dessaignes's *Frontières humaines*.

7   For more on the significance of water and the sea in Cahun and Moore's work, see Hannah Freed-Thall, *Modernism at the Beach: Queer Ecologies and the Coastal Commons*, New York: Columbia University Press, 2023, pp.22–24, and Amelia Groom, "In the Arms of the Sea: Claude Cahun and Marcel Moore at the Water's Edge," in *The 24th Biennale of Sydney: Ten Thousand Suns* (exhibition catalogue, 2024), pp.311–320.

8   For an analysis of Cahun and Moore's work as a theorization of trans nonbinary consciousness, see Jordan Reznick, "Through the Guillotine Mirror: Claude Cahun's Photographic Theory of Trans Against the Void," *Art Journal* (81:3, 2022), pp.53–69.